PARENT
PEP TALKS

PARENT
PEP TALKS

[**THE 10 MENTAL SKILLS**
YOUR CHILD MUST HAVE
TO SUCCEED
IN SCHOOL, SPORTS, AND LIFE]

JUSTIN SU'A

PLAIN SIGHT PUBLISHING
AN IMPRINT OF CEDAR FORT, INC.
SPRINGVILLE, UT

ISBN 13: 978-4621-1284-5

Published by Plain Sight Publishing, an imprint of Cedar Fort, Inc.
2373 W. 700 S., Springville, UT 84663
Distributed by Cedar Fort, Inc., www.cedarfort.com

Cover design by Angela D. Olsen
Cover design © 2013 by Lyle Mortimer
Typeset by Whitney Lindsley

Printed in the United States of America

10 9 8 7 6 5 4 3 2 1

THIS BOOK IS DEDICATED TO . . .

MELISSA
YOUR LOVE AND SUPPORT INSPIRES
AND EMPOWERS ME.

JAROM, MYA, AND ELIANA
YOU THREE TEACH ME HOW TO BE A
BETTER FATHER EVERY DAY.

MOM AND POPS
FOR TEACHING US CHILDREN THAT
NOTHING IS IMPOSSIBLE.

CONTENTS

CONTENTS

ACKNOWLEDGMENTS

I WOULD LIKE TO THANK MY WIFE AND KIDS FOR being so supportive while I wrote this book. Many times piggy-back rides were momentarily delayed so I could write for a few more minutes.

I want to express loving appreciation to my friends and family around the world. Your love, support, and encouragement continue to propel me to want to be better and to serve more.

I'm grateful to my academic mentors, who believed in me from day one.

Cedar Fort Publishing, thank you for allowing me the opportunity to share my message with the world. I couldn't have done it without you!

PREGAME PEP TALK

I WAS NEAR DALLAS, TEXAS, AND HOURS FROM DELIVERing a presentation on mental conditioning to a group of people who came from around the country for this conference. I was sitting in my hotel room, trying to sort through all the madness that was happening in my life; the *last* thing I was thinking about was the presentation I was going to be giving in a few hours.

Frustration was setting in because the things I wanted to do were being swallowed up by the things I had to do, and I didn't have things figured out. I had decided to use some of my downtime to create a sense of order in my mind when I received a call from a dear friend.

My initial thought was to call him back later—I had too much to do—but I found myself reaching for the phone anyway. Before I share with you how this brief conversation went, let me tell you about this guy on the other line. He's a former Ranger–qualified infantry officer who served with the 19th Special Forces Group, and his combat time with the 4th Infantry Division was the initial invasion of Iraq. As you could probably imagine, mental toughness is not something my friend lacks.

He shared with me that on Sunday of the previous week, he had a feeling that he should have asked me if I needed help with anything. I assured him that on Sunday things were fine, but that *today* (Tuesday), things were stressful. He told me to call him when I returned home so he could come over to offer some assistance. After expressing my appreciation, I told him that I had to go because I was in the middle of something. Before we finished, he said, "One more thing. Before I see you again, this is what I want you to do: **Go get yourself a straw, and suck it up.**" That was exactly what I needed to hear.

As a trained professional in sport and performance psychology, I come across many coaches and parents barking out commands similar to the one my friend gave me: "Suck it up!"; "Relax!"; "Be confident!"; and so on. Nothing is inherently wrong with those instructions, but they can come with one big problem—kids don't know *how* to do those things.

We live in a day when youth sports aren't what they used to be. Every year children seem to be getting bigger, stronger, and faster; and while you used to be able to play many different sports leading up to high school, today's youth athletes are specializing as early as five years old! Travel teams are at an all–time high, and the competition has never been greater. With these conditions setting the tone, coaches and parents are more intense, the expectations put on the kids are high, and success is primarily being measured by wins and losses. For your child to be successful, you as parents are going to have to sacrifice time and money to put your children in programs that have a tradition of excellence and quality coaching.

Not only is the world of youth athletics evolving, but also the pressure to succeed in school and at home is ever changing. With the way sports, academics, and society are continuing to evolve, more attention is going to be given to the mental aspect of perfor–mance. It doesn't matter how talented or how much potential your children have. If they lack the ability to perform under pressure, trust their training, focus through distractions, or bounce back from setbacks, they will struggle against an opponent who is better pre–pared mentally.

I was working with a football player who had recently signed with an NFL team. He was somewhat frustrated because he wasn't experiencing the same success he had in college. He even said, "I'm doing the same things I did in college to be successful." I smiled and responded, "That's your problem. You're doing the *same* things." I continued, "In the NFL, *everyone* is fast, *everyone* is strong, and *everyone* knows the game, and many know the game a lot better than you. If you're going to take performance to the next level, you're going to have to take your mind—set to the next level."

To successfully rise to the demands that are put on your children's shoulders, they're going to need to learn some important mental skills that will serve them well inside and outside of the performance arena, and I believe there is no one better to teach it to them than you—Mom, Dad, Guardian, Leader, Teacher, or Coach.

The idea to write this book came to me as I was doing a "Parent Pep Talk" workshop in San Antonio, Texas, one Saturday afternoon. These workshops are designed to teach parents the same mental skills I use with the elite performers to enhance focus, relaxation, motivation, and confidence. I was standing in a room full of parents, teaching them the ten must—have mental skills to help their children succeed, and I was amazed at the feedback I received afterward! Parents came up to me and told me how the information they learned will help strengthen their relationships with their children and ultimately strengthen their families. That's when I told myself that I had to write a book.

This book is to give you some advice on how to strengthen your child's mental game. When your child fails, you as parents feel the pain as well, and, on some occasions, you feel it more than your child does. The strategies in this book are aimed to help you help your child do the following:

- Self—motivate

- Be more optimistic

- Develop a winning mind—set

- Set and achieve high expectations

- Relax under pressure

- Learn how to bounce back from failures

- Build and sustain confidence

- Enjoy the journey

- Be a leader

- Change

I invite you to make the activities and principles your own. I always tell my students that what I'm about to share might be completely different from what they grew up learning. Try it out before you dismiss it. Some of you might read this and say to yourself, "I already do this!" If that's the case, good for you! I encourage you to keep going. I'm always asked, "Justin, will mental conditioning help me perform better?" To which I *always* respond, "I don't know." You'll never hear me guarantee success, more wins, or an A on the test. However, if your child puts these principles into practice, he'll put himself in a position to be more calm under pressure, perform in the present, and control his emotions—all of which *can* lead to the results he's looking for.

This book is written to give you, as a parent, a toolbox of mental skills to share with your child at the right time. I don't expect you to share every skill with your child; the key is simplicity. It would defeat the purpose of this book if you tried to force your child to do every activity; we want your child to not overthink and perform more. Sometimes when we are excited about information that can help another person (particularly when it comes to our kids), we are inclined to drown them with information. As your new mental conditioning coach, I ask you to please not do this!

As you read the following chapters, my challenge to you is to remember the ultimate purpose of this book: **To help strengthen the most important team in the world—your family.**

TEACH YOUR CHILD TO SELF-MOTIVATE

ONE SATURDAY MORNING MY SON CAME RUNNING into the house, "Dad! Dad! Come outside. I gotta show you what I can do!" I dropped what I was doing and followed him into the garage, "What is it, son?" I inquired. He threw on his helmet and shouted, "I can ride my bike now!"

I was excited. My wife, Melissa, had tried for hours to teach little Jarom how to ride a bike, but the fear of falling was crippling him, and his loving mother had charged me with the task instead. If my little guy could pull this off, my bike−riding teaching skills would remain dormant.

After locking his helmet in place, he got on the bike and took off. Despite being on the verge of falling with each rotation, my son was doing it. He was actually riding his bike! He returned to our driveway, and as any proud father would do, I asked, "How did you do that, son?" His response was priceless: "I got tired of seeing my friends ride around without me."

A common question parents, coaches, and leaders ask is, "How can I motivate those I lead?" While this question is *good*, I'd like to suggest an even better question: "What can I do to create an environment that will help my children motivate themselves?" The problem many youth have these days is the fact that they rely too heavily on their parents, coaches, and teachers to "motivate" them to action, when in reality, it is their job to motivate themselves. But how can they do this? Let's start with a little background to what motivation is and what you can do about it to increase it in your child.

MOTIVATION IS . . .

Imagine having the car of your dreams delivered to your drive—way, only to realize that it doesn't have an engine. Could you imag—ine the frustration? It doesn't matter how fast, powerful, or beautiful this car looks; without an engine, this hunk of metal is nothing but eye candy to passersby—it's going nowhere.

I use this analogy to describe individuals with tremendous "potential" but who lack the motivation to excel. I don't care how fast, smart, or talented a person is; if he lacks motivation, he (like the car) is going nowhere. So as parents, we lovingly nudge, pull, tow, or do whatever we can to spark action, and many times this leads to a frustrated child and an exhausted parent.

Understanding the different levels of motivation may help you tailor your approach the next time you decide to have a motiva—tional intervention with your son or daughter.

MOTIVATION LEVELS

According to motivation researchers Edward Deci and Richard Ryan,[1] there are essentially five levels of motivation. Level one is called *rewards and consequences*, and the key objective for this level is *compliance*. If your child does *x*, he'll get *y*. Here are some examples: "If you do well today, I'll give you a treat"; "If you do your home—work, you'll get a good grade"; or "If you don't do what I say, you're going to pay the price." People are driven by rewards and conse—quences, so you might be thinking, "But, Justin, it works!" And I would agree with you. It does—but research shows that this only works in the short term. In the long run, rewards and consequences hinder their intrinsic motivation, make tasks less enjoyable, and cause people to expect a reward for doing that task down the road.

Level two is *guilt*—doing something because you feel guilty if you don't. Your child may feel, "Aw, man. I'd better do it because if I don't, I'm going to feel bad." Again, not inherently bad, but we're after a sense of control here, and if your child is doing something out of guilt, control is minimized.

Level three is to *do something for a better future or viewing it as important*. Now we're getting closer to intrinsic motivation! Being motivated to do something for a better future is your teenager saying, "I'm going to work harder at the gym because I know in the long run it's going to be better for me" or "I'm going to go to school and study hard now because in the long run it's going to help me later." They are choosing to engage in something difficult, not because they necessarily love the activity itself, but rather, they value what it's going to do for them in the long run. Therefore, they will *choose* to do the difficult thing. You might be thinking, "That sounds just like doing something for a reward or consequence." The big difference is twofold: (1) they know *why* they are doing the activity, and (2) they are choosing to do it.

Level four is to *do something because it's just what you do*. You have adopted some behaviors that have become habitual. For some, as crazy as it sounds, they go to the gym because it's just who they are and that's just what they do. They aren't after a reward, and it's not fear of a consequence—it's just what they do. This is the highest form of intrinsic motivation.

Now, last but not least, the highest motivation level is to *do something because you love it*; this is what we call intrinsic motivation. These activities include the things you would do if you had all the time in the world. What are some of those things for you? Many people will say going for a walk, cooking, talking with loved ones, and so on. When I sit down with my young athletes, I always ask, "Why do you play [insert sport]?" The number one answer is: "Because it's fun." I then invite them to remember that when the going gets tough. It's true that they might be going after a championship, that they want to be the best, or that they are striving to play in college or professionally; but ultimately they got into this sport because it's fun.

A PARABLE: "TELL ME HOW TO BE AS WISE AS YOU"

One day a young man sought out a wise old mentor and asked him to share how to acquire all the knowledge he had. The wise mentor obliged to the young man's inquiry and took him to the beach. Standing on the shore, the mentor wanted to make sure he fully understood the desires of his young admirer and asked, "What is it you want to know again?" "How to gain all of the knowledge you have!" the young man exclaimed. "I thought so," the old man gently answered. So he took his eager follower into the water, where the mentor proceeded to grab the back of the young man's head and slam his face into the cold sea. The young man struggled to breathe for a few seconds, then the mentor pulled his head out of the water and asked, "What is it you want?" "To know how you acquired your wisdom," the young man said with his eyes squeezed shut because of the burning sensation of the salt water. The wise man wasn't pleased with the answer, so he thrust the young man's head back into the water. The young man fought for oxygen, and after a longer period of time, the mentor pulled him up again and asked, "What do you want?" "To know how you acquired—" The wise teacher threw his face into the water again before the young man could even finish his sentence. Now, this wasn't the experience the young man was expecting; he probably anticipated that his mentor would take his breath away—but not literally! Finally, the wise old man had compassion on his admirer's poor struggling soul, raised his head out of the water, and asked, "What do you want?" "Air! I want air!" the man shouted in panic. The mentor let go of the young man's head, and they walked together out of the water and back to the shore. Before the men parted ways, the wise mentor left his student with one morsel of knowledge: "When you want something as bad as you wanted air, you won't have to ask anyone how to do it."

One of the best mental skills your child can develop is the ability to self-motivate. Lasting motivation comes from inside. Your child must refuse to pawn off his motivation to someone else because once he makes *his* motivation your responsibility, or his teacher's or coach's responsibility, he relinquishes one of the most important things he needs to achieve excellence—control. He must be taught not to give people the keys to his motivation. That's his responsibility, not yours.

I don't care how big, fast, smart, beautiful, or any other adjective your child is, if he lacks motivation to put that potential into drive, he isn't going anywhere. Motivation is the engine that drives your child's performance. Here's how to help him develop more of it.

HOW DO YOU HELP YOUR CHILD DISCOVER WHAT HE REALLY WANTS?

Before I answer this question, let me ask you to recall a time your child was sincerely motivated. Can you remember how his motivation affected his focus, effort level, and drive to succeed? Well, chances are, when he was at his motivation peak, he had three things working for him. I call these the **Three Cs**: competence, control, and camaraderie.

COMPETENCE

Competence is your child's perceived skill level and ability to get the job done. One sure way your child's motivation will decrease is if he does everything he can to be successful but doesn't see progress—he wants to feel he's getting good at something. Perceived progression is a powerful motivator because as a child begins to work at it for a sustained amount of time, little by little he will get better, and the better he gets at something, the more enjoyable it becomes. And the more enjoyable it is, the more he's going to want to do it, and the more he does it—you get the picture.

A way to measure your child's competence is to keep score. Every day your child has the opportunity to enhance his competence in some way; just help him see that growth. The problem many parents run into is that they only measure results (grades, the final score, batting averages, and so on). The key is to measure progress; the small things that make a big difference.

I had the opportunity to work with a young cheerleader who

couldn't do a back handspring because she was afraid that she would get injured (a common fear many cheerleaders have). After talking with her, I learned that she would do it on her trampoline and parents' bed, but not on the actual spring floor she performs on. Rather than focusing her inability to execute on the spring floor, we shifted her focus on celebrating the successes. Every time she did her back handspring on her trampoline or parents' bed, I had her put a marble into a glass jar. On our next scheduled appointment, she walked into the gym with a jar full of marbles. We poured them out and counted each one—there were 110 marbles! I asked, "Do you know what this means?" She responded, "It means I can do it!" A little while later, she came up to me at one of her competitions and said, "Mr. Justin! I can do my back handspring now!"

For the child who struggles in school, focusing on getting straight A's might be such a long shot that he won't even try. However, if you measure every assignment he turns in on time or every day he completes his homework, you begin to measure something he can control, which will enhance his perceived competence, and that leads to greater motivation.

Strengthen your child's competence by keeping score of the things that define success for *him*. The moment he defines success and measures it, he takes competence into his own hands.

CONTROL

Your child wants to feel a sense of control. The moment he feels a loss of control, his motivation diminishes. I was working with a teenager once, let's call him "Seth," and I made one of his assignments to go and do something nice for his parents without them telling him to. One day while Seth was playing Xbox, he thought it was the perfect time to complete the mission. He put down the video game controller and headed over to the kitchen to wash the dishes. All of a sudden, his mom yelled from upstairs, "Hey, Seth, go wash the dishes!" As you could probably imagine, Seth's motivation to wash the dishes dropped immediately! I asked, "But, Seth, buddy, you were about to wash the dishes. Why did your motivation go down?" His answer parallels what the research says in motivation theory: "Because Mom made me do it."

Here is a key to motivation: When we feel a sense of control, motivation is enhanced. Help your child identify what he has control over. Help your child control what he can control—what his attitude will be after he misses a shot, how hard he studies, and so on—and help him be aware of falling into the trap of being too focused on the things that are largely out of his hands—what the coach thinks about him, the assignments their teacher gives them, and so on. His motivation will be enhanced as soon as he realizes that he can control his definition of success, his own effort, his focus, and his actions and reactions to adversity. As he understands that he has more control than he realizes, he will be more likely to motivate himself.

CAMARADERIE

Motivation will increase when your child is surrounded by greatness. In each of our brains, we have something called "mirror neurons," which make us more likely to behave in the same manner as those we associate with. Your child is more likely to display more effort, be more focused, and effectively respond to adversity (all signs of motivation) if he sees what it looks like on a daily basis. Now here's the thing: don't count on your child getting this at school, on his team, or with his band; the best camaraderie is the unity he feels within the walls of his own home.

A father and his son came to see me once. The dad was frustrated with his kid's performance on the baseball field and wanted to do everything possible to help him perform better. To kick off our first mental conditioning session, I asked the dad why he brought his son. "Well, Justin, my son is struggling to play baseball, and he doesn't look happy anymore. I don't want him to be so hard on himself. I love him, and it really doesn't matter if he strikes out, loses, or if he rides the bench. I just want him to be happy." I could see the sincerity of this father's words in his eyes. I turned to his teenage son, who was now looking down, and asked, "Okay, buddy, tell me: why are you here?" After about five seconds of silence, the boy looked up and had tears rolling down his cheeks. "I've never heard my dad say that before. The reason I play baseball is because he wants me to, and I get so nervous that he'll get mad at me if I don't do good." His father had no idea his son was interpreting the situation like this. The father said, "I'm sorry, son. You don't have to play baseball if you don't want to. I thought it was your choice. I'll love you either way." His son told him that just knowing this will help him be more calm and have more fun playing. After witnessing this three–minute loving conversation between a father and a son, I chuckled and said, "I think we have things settled here." I never saw those two again.

Children want to feel like they matter, that their voices and opinions are taken into consideration. If they have a sense of cama–raderie on their teams, in their classrooms, and especially in their homes, they are more likely be more motivated.

HELPING YOUR CHILD DISCOVER HIS MOTIVATION

As I said at the beginning of this chapter, it's your child's job to motivate himself, but it's the parents' job to create the environment for this to happen. I'll never forget my first day of graduate school. The professor in my motivation theory class posed the question, "What motivates you?" I knew exactly what it was! I wrote down my passion for helping people, making a difference in the world, being a great husband and father; the list went on and on. Many people, however, have no idea what their passion is, have no drive for improvement, and don't know where to start. Some of these people have motivation, but they haven't discovered it yet.

This happened to me one day when I was running out the door to deliver a presentation to a university baseball team. I realized I didn't have my keys, so I ran back into the house to look in the drawer where I normally put them. They weren't there. I ran to the clothes I wore the day before and checked all the pockets—no luck. My wife and kids sprung to action and helped me hunt them down. My heart began to race, my breathing rate increased, and I started to catastrophize: "What if I'm late? This is going to look so unprofes–sional that they'll never invite me back!" As I was running down–stairs, I found them. I didn't want to reveal to Melissa (my wife) where they were, so I just hollered at her from downstairs, "I found them, sweetheart! See you when I'm done! Thanks!" She asked the question I was trying to avoid, "Where did you find them?" Trying to dodge the question, I repeated, "Thanks, babe, I'll see you later." Again, she inquired, "Okay, but where were they? Were they in your pocket?" "No," I sheepishly answered, "they were in my hand."

The keys were in my hand the entire time! It was an embarrassing moment that I'm willing to share because it teaches a valuable principle: Sometimes the thing we are looking for is in our hands, but we just haven't discovered it yet. The same holds true with motivation. Your child may have something he is passionate about but has yet to discover his motivation. Here are two questions you can ask him to assist in this process.

QUESTION #1: WHY DO YOU DO WHAT YOU DO?

I heard an exchange between a college softball coach and one of his players. The player was noticeably frustrated and didn't want to finish the drill the coach was having her do. He assured her that she would be finished if she did one last thing—to tell him *why* she did certain things. "Why do you step that way? Why does your shoulder go here? Why don't you open sooner?" With each question her coach asked, the player responded the same way, "I don't know. That's just how I do it." He wasn't going to let her off the hook, so he kept peppering her with questions until she could explain her reasoning. Like a popcorn kernel, the heat was too much, and she popped by yelling, "I don't know why I do anything, coach!" Those who were close (including myself) wanted to see how this coach was going to respond to this blatant behavior of disrespect; he calmly walked up to her, pointed at her, and said a phrase I'll never forget, **"When you discover why you do what you do, you'll have more power to do it."**

This coach isn't a performance psychologist, but he knows about human performance, and he knows how motivation can impact a person. The reason your child may be going through the motions, feeling overwhelmed, or lacking purpose might be because he doesn't wake up each day with a reason *why*. If your child is an athlete, make sure he knows why he is going to practice on his way out the door. When he goes to school, help him understand *why* homework matters. I'm not saying that knowing why your child should do something is the ultimate answer to life's problems and he will be more motivated than ever before, but I am saying that when your child discovers why he does what he does, he will have more power to do it.

Activity: Pull out a sheet of paper and make two lists. Title one list "Love to do" and title the other "Have to do." Next to each item, help your child discover the "why" behind that activity. This is going to be particularly helpful for the things your child feels he has to do.

QUESTION #2: HOW DO YOU WANT TO BE REMEMBERED DOING WHAT YOU DO?

A fellow performance psychologist once told me that she was asked to write her own eulogy for one of her assignments. She couldn't believe the insight it provided her as to how she would like to be remembered. Answering this question caused her to reflect on her life and identify not only what really mattered in her life but also, more important, whether she was giving her time to those things.

Try this activity: Imagine yourself being at a banquet—a banquet dedicated to you. We've invited hundreds of people comprising the people you work with, who you went to school with, old teammates, and family. At a certain point, people are going to be invited to walk up on stage and share what makes you special. *What do you want them to say about you? How do you want to be remembered?*

What you want them to say helps you identify what your values are, helps you realize what matters to you, and gives you a foundation of motivation from which you will build your life. You can do the same for your children. Rather than allow the world to define success for them, ask *them* what defines success for *them*. As a loving parent, you'll probably see that your children would aim lower than you would like, and of course you will gently help them aim higher, but be careful not to push your goals on them. Let them take charge.

I once did the "banquet" activity with one of my athletes, and as he was writing down how he wanted to be remembered, he had an epiphany. I asked, "What is it?" He sheepishly responded, "I'm not living up to this person."

True motivation will be manifested in your children when they are true to themselves, define their own success, and live up to the values they truly believe in.

Activity: Have your child grab a sheet of paper. Then say, "I want you to imagine yourself at a banquet—a banquet dedicated to you. At this special event we've invited your friends from school, teachers, teammates, people you played against, and your family. At a certain point, everyone is going to have the chance to say what they think about you. Now write down your answer to these two questions: What do you want them to say about you? How do you want to be remembered?"

NOTE

1. E. Deci and R. Ryan, eds., *Handbook of Self-Determination Research* (Rochester, NY: University of Rochester Press, 2002).

TEACH YOUR CHILD HOW TO FLEX THE OPTIMISTIC MUSCLES

I CAN'T STAND WHEN PEOPLE COMPLAIN. HOW DO you like that for an opening statement to this chapter? But really, don't you hate it when you are trying to see the bright side of a situation, but "Negative Nancy," "Pessimistic Peter," "Grumpy Gary," or "Dark Cloud Deborah" (sorry if any of you have those names) takes it upon him− or herself to point out everything that is going wrong? If you want to teach your children an invaluable skill at a young age, teach them how to be more optimistic—emphasis on *teach*.

A common problem your children face is that they're too hard on themselves! It's much easier for them to identify what they lack, where they need to improve, and what they're not good at. They give power to what they focus on, so if they're wasting time focus−ing on all the reasons they're horrible at what they do, there's not much room for anything else. Their inability to be optimistic or to identify their strengths can lead to frustration, depression, and diminished motivation.

GRUMPY GIRL

I taught high school students for five years while I was pursuing my graduate degree, and I'll never forget an experience I had with one of my students, Sarah. As a teacher of youth and because of certain opportunities, I've been fortunate enough to meet thousands of teenagers arcross the country. Many of them are bright eyed, goal oriented, and happy to be alive; Sarah was the complete opposite of that. She rarely smiled, didn't speak to her peers, and initially refused to greet me with a handshake. As the semester progressed, I did everything I could to get to know her, but to no avail. I don't want to say that I gave up, but I was beginning to wonder if developing a friendship with Sarah was even possible.

One day she walked into class holding a green notebook, as grumpy as ever. She placed it on her desk and peppered me with her piercing stare throughout the class as she would normally do. During the hour, I saw her do something I've never seen before. She opened up that green notebook and wrote something. I thought that I must have said something insightful to get her to write it down! A few minutes later, she did it again! As the days passed, Sarah kept writing in that mysterious green notebook of hers and was changing. She started to open up to her peers and me, was more active and engaged in class, and began to smile.

A few months passed, and I didn't even recognize who this young woman had become. I was so fascinated by this dramatic change that I had to ask her the root of this transition. "Sarah, can I ask you a personal question?" I inquired. "Sure!" she answered. I asked, "What happened to you?" "What do you mean?" she asked. "You know, you've changed. I just want to find out how," I responded. With an inquisitive look on her face, she shot back, "I don't know what you're talking about." I didn't know if she was joking or if she really had no clue as to what I was saying. I decided to take a different approach. "Your green book. Tell me about it." "Oh, my *gratitude* book?" I smiled. "Gratitude book? Yes—tell me about that please." She went on to tell me that about two months previously her father went into her room and told her that she had a bad attitude and that she should change it. She stopped mid story and asked,

"Did you think I had a bad attitude two months ago?" Talk about awkward! I deflected the question by ignoring it. "So, tell me about the book." "Oh, sorry—back to my story . . ." she responded. I dodged a bullet! She told me that her dad told her that if she wanted to change her bad attitude, she needed to be more grateful. He gave her that green notebook and told her to carry it with her and write down all the things that come to her mind that she's grateful for. Over time, she stopped focusing on what was wrong in her life and began to give her attention to what was right—everything changed from that point on.

Your child might be struggling because she is failing to flex her optimistic muscles, and the reason she is struggling to do so isn't because she can't, but because she doesn't know how. Here are three things you can do to help your children flex their optimistic muscles:

HELP YOUR CHILD SEE BRIGHT SPOTS

When your children are struggling, they cannot see things as they really are. Their successes, as small as they may be, fall into their blind spots and aren't even noticeable to them. You need to be keenly aware of what your children are doing well because as you catch them doing those things and take notice, they'll begin to see the good things too. After every performance, ask your child to share with you her "bright spot" for that performance. The more she does it, the better she will get.

It's not easy being a youngster these days. With bullying more prevalent than ever before and with the strong notion that we need to be bigger, stronger, faster, prettier, smarter, and better than the next person, it is difficult for kids be optimistic when they are not measuring up. It's one thing not to live up to the world's expectations, but it's even more difficult to feel that you are letting down Mom and Dad. Help your children see the good.

THE OPTIMISTIC SOLDIER

I'll never forget an exchange I had with a soldier in the US

Army, who went to fight for our country as a man standing six feet three inches and weighing over 230 pounds; however, after an unfortunate incident, he woke up in the hospital weighing less than 100 pounds, mainly because he lost both of his legs and his left arm—he was now a triple amputee. While an improvised explosive device (IED) might have claimed his limbs, it didn't disable his optimism. I asked him, "How do you stay so positive amid adversity?" His response was simple yet powerful, "I always tell myself, 'It can always be worse.'" I smiled and quietly repeated, "'It can always be worse'? You think that?" He started to laugh and said, "Yeah! At least I'm right-handed!"

Your child wants to perform better, and if she is going to perform better, she must learn how to see the bright side of things. Your child gives power to what she focuses on, and focusing on the negative is not the way to go. Occasionally I'll have someone tell me, "Justin, I disagree. We all need some pessimism in our lives." I couldn't disagree more. A tried-and-true pessimist sees the world as the glass *always* half empty, and there is *nothing* they can do about it. Under that definition, we can do without a pessimistic mind-set. However, I can see what someone might mean by acknowledging the bad with the good; that I can agree with, and I'll actually be saying more about that later in this chapter.

"DADDY, CAN YOU TUCK US IN?"

At the end of each day, I make it a point to tuck all three of my children into bed at night. The routine is simple. I ask them, "What was something good that happened to you today?" "What did you learn today?" and "What is something you are going to do better tomorrow?" I love to hear my kids describe the "bright spots" they saw in their day. Some of their highlights have been coloring with a pink crayon, sitting on the stairs and talking, or seeing a bunny. It doesn't take much to work the optimistic muscle. It's a simple process, but for many it's not easy.

Activity: At the end of the day, have your children share with you the "bright spots" of their activities. You can even do this after their day at school, practice, or a game. The principle is simple: the better your children get at seeing the good, the more optimistic they'll be.

TEACH YOUR CHILD HOW TO REFRAME HER SITUATION

One of my favorite commercials of all time is one about optimism done by the Foundation for a Better Life. It depicted a young boy who was about nine years old standing at home plate on an empty baseball field. With a baseball in his left hand and his bat in his right hand, he shouted out, "I'm the greatest hitter in the world!" He threw the ball in the air and took a mighty swing. The ball missed the bat and fell to the ground—strike one. Unfazed, the little boy picked up the ball and shouted even louder, "I'm the greatest hitter in the world!" He took another tremendous swing, only to come up empty a second time. "Strike two," he mumbled.

Now, noticeably worried, he did what the big leaguers do—adjusted his hat and spat in his hands. After taking a deep breath, and now with two strikes on him, he shouted once again, "I'm the greatest hitter in the world!" The ball went into the air, and just like the previous two attempts, his athletic prowess was no match for the pull of gravity on the ball. "Strike three?" the boy said, shocked. After a moment of hesitation, his eyes lit up, a smile graced his face, and it hit him, "I'm the greatest *pitcher* in the world!"

I love the statement "When you change the way you look at things, the things you look at change." If you want to help your child be more optimistic, teach her how to look at her situation through the lenses of effectiveness. The stressful situation your child is experiencing or the fear she is feeling isn't necessarily a result of the event itself but rather her interpretation of the event.

THE DANCER MIND-SET

I was working with an elite dancer, Rachel, who was sabotaging herself because of the way she was interpreting each of her performances. When you are performing at the level Rachel was, it's hard not to let perfectionism get the best of you; and that was the case with her. "I want to win!" was the reason she wanted to perform well. She spent hours with her dance teachers, and her parents were investing a lot of money for her to receive the quality of training she was getting, so it's easy to see the pressure she was putting on herself. She described success as something that she *had* to do, *expected* to do, and she would not accept failure—there's where her problem was. She wanted it so badly that it was hurting rather than helping her. The more she wanted perfection, the harder it was to acheive because it increased anxiety and lead to tense muscles and a decrease in energy and focus—not a good recipe for success.

As we worked together, we tried to change one thing: being a more optimistic thinker by learning how to reinterpret her performances in a manner that will help rather than hurt her. Instead of viewing a performance as an opportunity to prove her worth or to show the world how great she was—which was causing tremendous stress—we wanted her to view it in a way that would help her be more relaxed, have more fun, and just dance. This was a more optimistic approach. It didn't take long before she realized that she wanted to focus more on having fun and less on results—this changed everything.

The elite dance world is filled with critical judging, expectations for precision, and a tendency to demand perfection, all of which are not necessarily conducive to producing a relaxed dancer. However, the dancers with the right mind-set are able to focus through those distractions and give their attention to having fun and focusing on the process rather than the results. At this moment, Rachel decided to be one of those dancers. In a conversation she and I had nearly two years after our initial meeting, she told me that the shift in her mind-set was something that helped her take her dancing to the next level.

Activity: Teach your child how to master the art of looking at things differently. Invite your child to answer the following:

- How can this situation make you stronger?

- What is the lesson you can learn from this experience?

- How do you think this can help you in the long run?

- What are you going to do about it?

As your child answers these questions, it helps her change her mind-set from "why me?" to "what now?"

TEACH YOUR CHILD TO LOOK OBSTACLES IN THE FACE

Too many people have the notion that optimism is just about positive thinking, smiley faces, rainbows, skipping, princesses, uni—corns, and just "believing" everything is going to work out dandy (okay, maybe I got a little carried away). But the reality is, optimism is acknowledging a difficult situation including all of the obstacles and hardships it entails, identifying what you're going to do about it, and then executing the plan. Optimistic people are not oblivious to the fact that adversity is inevitable, the road will be difficult, and failure is likely. However, while the pessimist complains about why it's not going to work out, focusing on the probabilities, the realistic optimist is going to focus on what they want to happen and what they are going to do about it—they focus on the possibilities. This can be learned.

Build your child's optimism by teaching her to expect setbacks, learn from them, and have a plan on how to get back up *when* she falls. Help her realize that she can fail without feeling like a failure. The less your child fears failure, the more likely she can learn from it. One of the main reasons your child struggles to see the good is that she is expecting perfection, and on many occasions, the need to be perfect is a message that is being sent from parents, teachers, and coaches.

OUR INITIAL MEETING

Anytime I sit down with my students for the first time, I tell them that we don't have time to waste, so I need to get to know them as well as possible, as fast as possible. I tell them not to hold back two things from me: what they're good at and what they're afraid of. After sharing their strengths, I ask them to share their true weaknesses and their deepest fears (when it comes to performance). You would probably be surprised to know that professional athletes and elite performers fear the same things your nine-year-old child does: failure, letting people down, messing up, and what other people think.

After I know what they are good at and what they fear, I ask what they want. "What is a specific and challenging goal you want to accomplish?" I inquire. After they tell me, I pull out their list of fears and say something like this:

"On your way to greatness, I hope you realize that you're going to have to look each one of these fears in the face. You may get injured. You might not achieve your goal as fast as you would like, and you might have to sacrifice a lot of things that you love to do in order to achieve excellence. It's going to be hard, and you will experience physical, mental, and emotional pain on your way to your destination. You won't be perfect. You'll mess up over and over again. Now, knowing all this before your journey begins, *is this still something you want to do?*"

The majority of my students give me a resounding "yes!" while others are a little more hesitant with their answer. The purpose of me doing this at the outset is to help my students maintain optimism through adversity by acknowledging that adversity is inevitable. When it comes to performance, no one likes unexpected setbacks. They can take the wind out of your sails, but if you teach your child to expect difficult things to happen, he or she will be more likely to maintain a good attitude.

As you instill the skill of developing and flexing your child's optimistic muscles, she will not only reap the benefits on the playing field, dance floor, or classroom, but, most important, she will also be more optimistic, which will have a positive impact where it matters most—in your home.

Activity: Help your child make a list of things she is good at and things she fears (make it performance specific). Then ask her

[24]

to share with you a specific and challenging goal she wants to accomplish in the near future pertaining to that performance. Help your child to understand that in order to achieve this, she will come face-to-face with many of her fears. Assure her that she can do it, and although she can't control what happens to her, she can control how she chooses to respond.

[MENTAL SKILL #3]

TEACH YOUR CHILD HOW TO HAVE THE RIGHT MIND-SET

YOUR CHILD'S MIND-SET IMPACTS EVERYTHING. HIS mentality for homework will affect how well he does with his homework, and the mentality he has on the golf course is different than the one he has asking someone out on a date. In this chapter I share principles you can use to help your child shape his mind-set so it will help and not hurt him.

LESSON LEARNED

One of the most important things I've learned from working with people from different walks of life is that high–level athletes don't have the market cornered on performing under pressure. Your child has people counting on him as well and is expected to get the job done!

Life is far from easy for the youth of these days, and they have so many things that take a hit on their confidence, pull their focus, and increase their stress levels. The purpose of this chapter is to give you tools to help your child get out of his own way to perform at a high level—whatever the performance may be (music, school, dancing, sports, and so on).

MIND-SET MATTERS

Your child must understand that mind–set matters, and he chooses his mind–set! Once he understands these principles, he is going to have the edge walking into any circumstance, having increased confidence to succeed.

HABIT DEVELOPMENT

A dangerous mind–set trap your child can fall into is fixating too much on results. To help your child achieve great results in sports, school, and life, help him focus on developing high–performance habits rather than focusing on results. If your child wants to get better grades, it's important to not only decide what GPA he is shooting for but to also identify the study and classroom habits it's going to take to achieve those results.

I was working with a high school student once who wanted to improve his test scores, and to do that, he identified one habit that would help him feel more prepared going into each test: finish his homework assignments. He had the tendency to turn in his assignments incomplete because he would think about all the other things he could be doing. He knew that if he committed to finishing his homework assignments, it would affect his test scores, and it did!

Activity: Ask your child to complete the following sentence, "If I had the habit of [insert habit], I would be better at [insert type of performance]." Then identify how you can work together to help the child develop this habit. Help him understand that it won't be easy and may take a long time; however, in the long run, it will help make consistent progress toward his goals.

PERFORMANCE MAPP

Okay, now we're going to talk about the performance MAPP. It all starts with your child's *mentality*; this comprises his thoughts and deliberate self−talk. The things he thinks and says to himself will influence his *affect* (that's just a fancy way of saying "emotions")— our thoughts impact our emotions. Your child's emotions will then influence how he feels *physically*, which will ultimately impact his *performance*. How he regulates this process will have a tremendous impact on how well he performs, and how he performs will in turn and influence his mind−set.

Your child's performance MAPP could be helpful or harmful, and it all depends on what he chooses to make of it. A harmful performance MAPP begins with the self−talk, "I can't stand this!" This can be an example of a harmful mentality your child may have toward doing something. If thoughts of "I can't stand this!" are flooding his mind, what do you think that's going to do to his emotions? He is obviously going to be angry. Now you may be able to put the rest of the puzzle together. These emotions are going to lead to tight muscles, low effort, and maybe even an increased heart rate, which may lead to a subpar performance. But it doesn't end there! The results to his performance will give evidence to the initial thought of "I can't stand this!" which will then solidify this harmful performance MAPP he had created for herself.

So how does your child break this cycle? It starts with his mentality. Let's begin with what he says to himself. Rather than succumb to self−sabotage, he needs to try fueling his mind with phrases, pictures, and words that will empower him, such as "I've got this!" When he is thinking this, chances are excitement and joy follow closely behind. When he's feeling these emotions, he is more inclined to give more effort, feel more positive energy, or even feel more relaxed. A mind full of effective thoughts will help him regulate his emotions, help his body feel loose, and put himself in a great position to have an effective performance. It doesn't guarantee a successful performance, but it puts him in the best position to be at his best.

This is an important concept to understand: Mentality matters! What your child thinks drives his emotions, which influences his behavior, and that ultimately impacts his performance. Just being aware of this gives him the edge.

TWO PRINCIPLES

Now that we identified the importance of focusing on habit development and regulating the performance MAPP, I'll close this chapter by sharing two principles you can use to help your child develop an effective mind–set to tackle whatever he does.

PRINCIPLE 1: THE MORE YOUR CHILD BELIEVES A THOUGHT TO BE TRUE, THE MORE AUTHORITY IT HAS OVER HIM

Teach your child to refuse to be a person who allows his own thoughts to bully him around. Unknowingly, he may be hinder–ing his performance because of the ineffective thoughts he allows to sink in. The more your child continues to replay thoughts such as, "I'm not good," "I'm terrible," "I'm the worst," and other self–sabotaging thoughts, the more he will tend to believe them. These thoughts give power to what your child focuses on, and the more he focuses on a thought, he will begin to believe it's true. Research shows that we have approximately 50,000 thoughts a day—and 80 percent of those thoughts are negative!

The first step your child needs to take in conquering this inef–fective thinking is to *acknowledge* those harmful thoughts. The moment he thinks change is impossible, exaggerates a setback, or fears failure, he needs to catch himself. After he acknowledges the ineffective mind–set, he can choose to debate those performance–sabotaging thoughts with more effective ones.

Your child probably knows a thing or two about debating, and chances are that he's had many instances to be in a debate or two. Which restaurant is the best, why one music artist is better than another, or which sports team is the best are common topics that youth may have debated before.

To successfully win these pointless debates, children are sure to gather evidence to support their position and carefully listen for flaws to their opponent's reasoning. Even if they're wrong, they don't admit it! Now they need to apply those same principles to conquering their ineffective mind–set.

Your child may fall victim to allowing his negative self–talk to beat himself up without even putting up a fight! He may have rec-curring thoughts that are hindering his performance, but he hasn't taken any thought to debate it. He has the power to answer an inef-fective thought with "No, that's not true!"

Your son may be trying out for the basketball team when the thought "I might not make the team" creeps in. Rather than let that thought run wild in his mind, he can debate it with, "You know what? I can't control if I make it or not, but I practiced every day for this moment, and I'm going to go out there and trust my training." Or you can say, "I might not make it, but I'm going to give it a shot. What do I have to lose?"

As your child develops the ability to debate ineffective thoughts, this is going to keep him from effecting his emotions, behaviors, and ultimately his performance. Your child can take control of his performance by taking control of what he thinks about.

Activity: Have your child write down two ineffective thoughts he has a tendency to believe. Help him come up with strong evidence to debate those thoughts when they pop up again.

PRINCIPLE 2: YOUR CHILD IS A PRODUCT OF THE DECISIONS HE MAKES

We make thousands of decisions every day, and once we take control of the decisions we make, we're going to be able to take control of our performance. Unbeknownst to many of us, we have much more power than we realize. We choose what to say, we choose what to think, and we can choose how to respond to any given situation. The danger of not being aware of the decisions we make is going on autopilot—we get so used to responding in a par-ticular way that it becomes our knee-jerk reaction, and we just react rather than choosing to respond.

Many people fall into the trap of blaming other people and cir-cumstances for the state of their situation—teach your child to avoid this. The key is to focus on what he can control and to proactively respond to the challenge and refuse to wallow in pity.

One of the best ways to make good decisions under pressure is to *decide early*. Many of the performers I work with are forced to make tough decisions under pressure (a quarterback expected to perform, a CEO with a tight deadline, a figure skater in the regional championships, and so on). Being prepared to make decisions in the heat of the moment begins *before* the heat of the moment.

What if my child doesn't do what he decides to do?

Good question! I get this all the time. I was working with a baseball player who made a decision to take batting practice every day. One afternoon I was talking to him on the phone, and he mentioned that he was going to take the day off because he was too tired. I said, "Okay, I don't see a problem with that. But I just want you to make sure that you are making a conscious decision not to do what you said you were going to do. Are you okay with that?" The young man paused for a moment and said, "I'm going to hit."

If your child is more conscious of the little decisions he makes, he'll be more apt to catch himself when he is being nudged to do something that is contrary to what he truly wants. Now, I'm not saying he's going to be perfect and *always* make good decisions! It's important for your child to remember to learn from those moments he has poor judgment, because the lessons learned make that process worthwhile.

As your child develops the ability to make good decisions consistently, his confidence will be enhanced.

Activity: Have your child write down two decisions he wants to commit to for the next week. Ask him why he chose those two things and how he expects committing to those decisions will be beneficial.

[MENTAL SKILL #4]

TEACH YOUR CHILD
TO AIM HIGH

MY MOM AND DAD ARE THE EPITOME OF THE CHASE-your–dreams mentality. My father didn't play baseball until college and was an All–American out of BYU and went on to play for the Los Angeles Dodgers and Milwaukee Brewers. After professional ball, he and my mother opened and ran a successful trucking company based out of Los Angeles.

As we were growing up in the Su'a household, our parents would always tell my sister, my brother, and me that we could do anything we wanted, and nothing was out of the question. They let us have our own dreams, and it didn't matter whether I wanted to be a cowboy, ninja, football player, or the next MC Hammer— Mom and Dad were supportive.

People always ask, "Did your parents make you play baseball?" I always respond that my parents did not force me to play baseball, but they encouraged me to give basketball, golf, and other sports a shot. They wanted us to do what we loved and not what they loved—baseball just happened to be my passion.

The confidence my parents had in me helped me set high goals. The summer before my senior year in high school, I made a bold declaration in the privacy of my own room: "I'm going to be the

Daily Breeze Player of the Year." The *Daily Breeze* is a South Bay (California) newspaper that covers a tremendous population, so this was a pretty bold prediction coming from a kid who was playing above−average baseball but was not what you would call a "super−star." I didn't care. I wanted it, and I was willing do the work to achieve it. I grabbed a piece of paper and wrote my goal down, and then I decided to write down a few more things I wanted to accomplish: get a full−ride baseball scholarship and be a Division I All−American baseball player—I was riding the wave of high expec−tation. I knew I had a long way to go, so I got to work immediately.

I posted my goals up on my wall next to my door and told my parents what I wanted to do. I would wake up every morning at 5:30 to go to seminary (an early−morning Bible study class for the youth of my church), and upon returning home, I would go into the garage and hit off a tee into a net until it was time for school. I tried to be the first to practice and the last to leave. Our team topped the national baseball ranking charts. Despite an unfortunate loss in the California Interscholastic Federation (CIF) Championship, it was still a season to remember. When the smoke settled, I was awarded the *Daily Breeze* Player of the Year!

I entertained the opportunity to play for UCLA and California State University, Fullerton, but I opted to wear the jersey of the BYU Cougars, to follow the footsteps of my father. The mental−ity I had as a senior in high school went with me to Provo, Utah, and I was fortunate enough to help my team win the Mountain West Conference Championship that year, which was followed by a Freshman All−America Award after the season.

I don't share this story to boast; those who know me best will tell you that I don't feel comfortable receiving praise. The purpose of me sharing this about myself is to show you the tremendous impact my parents had on my ability and desire to excel. If you want to help your child succeed, you must teach her to aim high and rise above mediocrity.

HELP YOUR CHILD SOAR BY LETTING HER FALL

No one wants your child to succeed more than you do, but I've seen some parents who have such a tight grip on their children that these children don't have the ability to learn for themselves or experience failure. Many people don't aim high because of their fear of failure. If you want to help your child aim high, help her reinterpret failure. I've been rejected by graduate schools, had businesses deny my services, and have been criticized for what I teach. While these experiences hurt, I didn't allow them to disable me emotionally because of how I've been taught to look at failure—as an opportunity to learn.

When I was ten years old, I was playing in the equivalent of the Little League World Series, the World Series in the Mustang Division for the Pony Baseball Organization. I was on the mound with the game on the line against another rival California team out of Heart. I was in a jam, and my father, who was the coach, asked me to intentionally walk the batter with the bases loaded to create a force out at every base (ask someone who knows baseball to explain that to you if you're lost); this was something college baseball players and Major Leaguers do, but not a ten-year-old! In this situation, there is no room for mistakes, and as a young, mentally untrained boy, I wasn't prepared for the pressure. I walked the kid on four straight pitches and lost the game for us—we were eliminated.

Tears fell from my cheeks as I walked off the mound in defeat. Later that night as I lay in my bed and cried, my dad came into my room and told me how proud of me he was. He told me that I was the only one he would have put so much pressure on and that he was proud of how I did. He then told me of a time *he* experienced something similar when he played baseball in college. His team was playing against the University of Texas, and he struck out when everyone was counting on him. He then said, "Son, you'll get another chance someday." He was right. Not only did I get another chance to perform under pressure on the baseball field, but also I got the chance in the classroom and in my home. Although I was only ten years old, that experience is a milestone for me because I learned how to fail without my parents making me feel like a failure. You can do the same for your child.

Activity: Tell your child about a time you failed, and what you learned from it. Help her understand that failure is an opportunity to learn and grow, and that just because she hasn't been able to do something, it doesn't mean she can't.

ENOUGH WITH THE "YEAH, BUT . . ."

"I can do hard things" is one of the most important mind–sets you can help your child develop. On too many occasions, our youth are distracted by their perceived "hard road" (for example, bad test scores, physical injuries, missed opportunities, and failure). While each of these things can derail your child, they don't have to. If you want to help your child do something great, you've got to teach her to eliminate the "yeah, but . . ." from her vocabulary. Your child will *always* find an excuse or come across something easier to do. The thing that gets in the way of people performing to their potential is complaining; complaining leads to excuses for a poor performance.

LIVING THE DREAM

I once saw a double–leg amputee in a wheelchair struggling to enter a building. The door had a handicap–accessible button to press, which would automatically open the door, but he decided not to use it. Although I was already in the building, I was still too far away to help. I hustled to his assistance, thinking, "Why doesn't he just press the button?" On my way there, he tried to enter two more times, unsuccessfully; he would try to swing open the heavy glass door, but it would close on him before he had time to wheel himself inside. On his third attempt, he pulled the door, and rather than go straight in, he did a fancy spin–move and made it with ease. I was too late to help, but he saw my intention to run to his aid. He smiled and said, "Thanks for thinking about me!" I asked how he was doing, and his response was classic, "Living the dream, sir— living the dream."

This man could have complained about his situation and used it as an excuse to give up and wait for someone to solve his problems for him, but instead he took the initiative to figure out how to suc—ceed on his own. So teaching your child to conquer the habit of complaining will help her aim high and keep a "can–do" attitude.

Activity: Complaining and making excuses are like two peas in a pod. Help your child kick the habit of complaining by bring-ing awareness to it. For one day, have your child pay close attention to how many times she complains about something out loud. The first step to making a change is creating aware-ness. This might also be a good activity for Mom and Dad.

"RECALCULATING" DOESN'T MEAN "GAME OVER"

Another reason people don't aim high is because they don't want to set themselves up for failure. I once heard the story of a teenager who didn't want to apply to a certain university because she didn't think she would be able to handle the agony of being declined. Too many youth these days let the fear of not reaching their destination keep them from playing the game. When the global positioning system (GPS) in your car is saying "recalculating," that doesn't mean pull over and turn the car off because you're done; it means keep going and make an adjustment to get you back on track. Unfortu-nately, the "recalculating" times in our lives make people bitter, not better.

If you want to give your child the mental edge, teach her how to master her mind–set when she is in a situation that is not going according to plan. Things are easy when everything is turning out as expected; however, a person with the high–performance mind–set is able to be patient through the "recalculating" phases in life.

Could you imagine the success your child would have if she would learn how to not hit the panic button when things don't go her way? Does your child tend to throw in the towel when she perceives that "failure" is inevitable? That doesn't have to be the case—a recalculating phase can be an opportunity to find a new path and discover things never before realized. Just like those moments where you get "lost" on your way to a certain destination only to discover a favorite restaurant, a new shortcut, or a store that you've been looking for, those moments of being "lost" in life can prove just as beneficial—if you keep your head up and your eyes open.

A NEW CAREER

As I hit eleventh grade, my heart was set on what I was going to do: be a professional baseball player and a sports broadcaster. My college had an outstanding broadcasting department, and I was well trained to get into that field if baseball didn't work out. Well, not only did baseball not work out, but my four years of learning how to be on-air talent didn't grow into a career of providing people with highlights on SportsCenter. Instead, I chose a different route—performance psychology. Someone might have a case in saying, "Justin, you didn't achieve your dreams," but I love what I do for a living and wouldn't change it for the world. I guess I didn't know what I *really* wanted to be when I grew up—until I grew up.

As you teach your child to aim high, help her realize that her journey to her goal is going to be filled with unexpected twists, turns, and flat tires. Your child might not make the team, the coach may treat her unfairly, and she might suffer a devastating loss she will remember the rest of her life, but she must be taught that these setbacks don't mean she's a failure; and it doesn't mean *you're* a failure as a parent.

Some of you reading this are in a position you never thought you would be in—don't give up. Being in a "recalculating" phase of your life gives you the opportunity to see things you never would have seen, learn things you never would have learned, and meet people who are going to be key players as you continue on your journey to where you want to go.

Activity: If your child finds herself in a "recalculating" phase in life, ask her to focus on what she wants to happen, and what she's going to do about it.

MAKING IT HAPPEN VERSUS LETTING IT HAPPEN

Do you ever find yourself hoping for the best, visualizing success, and telling everyone how good things are going to be in the future, but you don't do a thing about it? For many, there is a void between success and execution. Many *say* they want success, hang the motivational posters, listen to the music, read the books, and watch inspirational movies, but they *miss* one important ingredient: *If you want to achieve great things, you've got to separate the things you need to make happen from the things you need to let happen, then act accordingly.*

People who think success will just happen to them without working toward it every day will find themselves feeling empty. On the other hand, there are some out there trying to force success, when the better way is to be patient and let things play out. If your child is struggling to perform the way she thinks she should, chances are she is trying to "let it happen" when she should be "making it happen," or the other way around.

LETTING IT HAPPEN

Many young performers lack patience these days, expecting success to happen because they put in a few hours of hard work. The sooner they learn that it doesn't work that way the better. When they try to force success, it increases anxiety and muscle tension, and it narrows their focus, thus making success more elusive. Trying to make something happen when you should be letting it happen is one of the most common pitfalls to young athletes today. Ultimately the things that your child needs to *let* happen are things that are out of her control (officiating, homework assignments, other dancers on the team, and so on).

HOW DO I "LET IT HAPPEN"?

As a pitcher, the more you try to force a pitch by gripping it too tight, aiming the throw, or trying to *make* the ball have movement, the less effective you'll be. The best pitchers trust their stuff.

Just like building trust in a friend or a loved one, your child must understand that meeting a goal takes time and consistency. Letting things happen means focusing on the things you can control and accepting the fact that you have no control over some things (we'll talk more about this later). One of the best ways to let it happen is to train well. When the pressure is on, and the game is on the line, there is only one way your child can trust her training and just let it happen: if she feels her practice prepared her for this moment.

Another way to let things happen is to let go of the results. Yes, I said to *let go of* the results! This is coming from someone who hates to lose—I'm so competitive that if you're running on the treadmill next to me, we are racing. Nothing is wrong with wanting to win, or even expecting to win; however, when it's showtime and you are in the middle of your test, the big game, or your dance concert, the last thing you should be thinking about is the outcome.Let it happen.

MAKE IT HAPPEN

We choose not to make things happen for many reasons: not enough time, too hard, too tired, procrastination, we want someone to do it for us, the timing isn't right, and every other excuse in the book. The reality is that if you say you want something and you don't do anything about it—news flash!—you don't really want it. We make time for the things that are important to us.

Making something happen requires time, tremendous effort, being uncomfortable, learning, growing, asking for help, and failing. I always have teenagers say, "But that sounds hard." To which I reply, "It is!" Aiming for greatness and getting there is not for the faint of heart or for those who just expect to be carried there; it takes pure hustle. Making something happen means focusing on what your child can control: what she focuses on, her attitude, her effort level, and her reaction to adversity.

HOW DO I HELP MY CHILD "MAKE IT HAPPEN"?

First of all, you help your child make it happen by teaching her what "it" is. The key to making things happen is to focus on controlling what she has control over. Teach your child to understand that she's a human being—an organism that *acts*, not an object that is acted upon.

I once worked with a professional involved in sales. This man was a wrestler in college and found himself struggling in his profession. He wasn't hitting his quotas or enjoying the environment, and, as a result, his performance was causing him to inch closer and closer to the chopping block. The problem wasn't his lack of competence; it was his mind-set. We discussed making things happen versus letting things happen, and we discovered that he wasn't taking things into his own hands. From that moment on, he decided that rather than let someone else get the job done, he was going to train to have the competence to do it himself—he decided to make it happen.

My last piece of advice for those of you teaching your child to aim high is to enjoy the ride! It's amazing to see the things people accomplish when they're having a blast doing what they do.

Activity: With your child identify the things she should let happen and compare them to the things she should make happen. Knowing the difference between the two is just the beginning, and acting accordingly is the key.

TEACH YOUR CHILD
HOW TO CALM DOWN

HOW DO YOU RESPOND TO UNDUE STRESS? YOU MAY respond one of many ways: yell at people, become quiet, make bad food choices, throw things, and so on. If you want to give your child a tool that will help him in every aspect of his life, teach him how to relax. This chapter is for those of you who have a child who performs well at practice but struggles during the game; or for your child who has all the answers in that brain of his, but when it's time to put it on paper for his big test, he has a hard time doing so because the anxiety is getting the best of him.

The mental skill to "relax" is one of the most common instructions parents and coaches give to their children or players. The only problem is that rather than saying it in a way that serves as a performance cue that actually reduces stress, they say, "HEY, JOHNNY! RELLLAAAXX!!" This is a sure way to push your child into a state of anxiety rather than relaxation. Parents and coaches set the energy tone for everyone else. If Mom and Dad are high–strung and stressed out at home, it's going to have a tremendous impact on the stress levels of the children; additionally, if the coaches are whining and complaining about every bad call from the referee, the players are going to follow suit, which will elevate the stress level on the team, and in many cases it will hinder performance.

I'll never forget a time I was pressing the panic button as a young high school pitcher. We were playing against a great team, and they were rocking me—some of the balls those guys hit still haven't landed yet. My father was one of the coaches, and he probably saw the frustration in my body language, so he called a well-needed time-out. As he walked to the mound, I thought, *Okay, good. Pops can tell me what I'm mechanically doing wrong so I can fix it and do better.* As my father approached the mound, he looked at me right in the eyes and asked, "Are you hungry, son?" I thought, *Did I just hear that right? Did he ask if I was hungry in the middle of this game?* My response was similar to what any young teenager would say in this situation: "Kinda." "What do you want to eat after the game?" he asked. I knew he was serious, so I told him. "A Whopper." He proceeded to ask me if I wanted cheese on it and then asked for my drink of choice. I told him that I did and that I would like a Dr Pepper. After rehearsing to me what he was going to order at Burger King, he said, "Okay, that's what we'll do after the game!" He then proceeded to turn around and walk off the mound, leaving me completely confused by this unexpected conversation. As he was walking back to the dugout, he took a second to look back at me, smile, and offer some words of encouragement. This was a father communicating to his son: "Relax, you can do this."

Coach Su'a knew that yelling at me wouldn't help, and filling my mind with mechanical cues wasn't going to prove beneficial, but getting me to relax my mind was going to do the trick—he was right. So, to help your child remain "as cool as the other side of the pillow," as ESPN anchor Stuart Scott likes to say, let me offer some principles that might help you along the way.

FOCUS ON THE CONTROLLABLE

Have you ever sat next to someone on a plane who talks too much, asks too many questions, and doesn't let you sleep? I'm that guy. It fascinates me to learn what makes people tick, and I find myself engaging in deep conversations with complete strangers. One day, I was on a plane from Salt Lake City, Utah, headed to Denver, Colorado, to speak. As I boarded the plane and situated myself in my seat, the lady occupying the window seat next to me was looking out the window. "What's taking you to Colorado?" I asked with genuine enthusiasm. To my surprise, the woman calmly gripped the arm rests, gave me an uncomfortable smile, showed rapid eye movement, and stuttered, "I—I'm going to be in a piano competition." This was a common case of the physiological effects of stress, and from that moment on and for the entire flight, she elaborated on why this competition was filling her with so much anxiety.

As we soared through the sky, she told me that three things in particular were causing the most stress: the judges, the other competitors, and performing in front of an audience. She knew that the judges were going to be hard on her since they had seen her before. Her competitors were some very talented performers coming from around the country to compete, and she wondered if she could compare. Finally, this was the first time she would compete in front of an audience and was afraid they would somehow influence the judges.

The flight attendant had invited us to get ready to land when my newfound friend realized something: she did all the talking! In an attempt to get to know me in a few minutes, she said, "I'm sorry, Justin. I've been rude talking this entire time. How about you? What do *you* do for a living?" I smiled and said, "I think you might be mad at me when I tell you what I do." "Mad? Why would I be mad because of your profession?" she asked. I said, "I'm a mental conditioning coach, and my job is to help people perform at a high level under pressure." She paused for a moment to digest what I just said, and a look of realization crossed her face. She replied, "What? That's what you do for a living? Then why didn't you help me this entire plane ride?" Although she said it in jest, I knew she was serious. I told her that a common strategy we use is to allow the performer to "let it all out." I wanted to be a sounding board for her. She thanked me for my kind gesture and added an invitation for anything else I might be able to add to help her anxiety. I told her that I would like to share a simple yet powerful principle with her that would serve her well in this situation. She opened a notebook and was ready to write. I told her, "Focus on what you can control and let go of the things you can't." We then spent the last few minutes identifying the things that were controllable and the things that needed to be let go. She came to the realization that the three things she was most worried about—the judges, competition, and audience—fell under the I–can't–control category, so she decided to shift her focus.

I don't know what happened to that woman, but as we were leaving the airplane, she assured me that she was going to keep this simple principle in mind and that it already helped her feel more relaxed.

It's a principle that you might find in a fortune cookie, but common knowledge isn't always common practice. As you help your child focus on what he can control, you're going to see his ability to calm his nerves will be enhanced because energy won't be wasted on things that cannot be changed.

Activity: With your child, identify the things in his performance he can and cannot control. Bringing awareness to these factors can take a tremendous load off his shoulders.

One final note before we move on to the next principle. Your child might fall into one of two categories: he feels he has absolutely no control over anything, or he feels he must control everything. These polar–opposite mind–sets can have the same effect on one's stress level: increase it. If your son feels that he is entitled to success or that success is something that is out of his control, help him identify specific things that he has control over. Little does he realize that he can control his interpretation of the situation, he can choose the attitude he's going to have, and he can even choose the actions he's going to take given his circumstance.

On the other hand, if your daughter is drowning in her pursuit of controlling everything in her life, have extra patience as you show her, in a gentle and sincere way, the things she cannot control, such as what other people think about her, the past, the future, and the decisions of others. Be aware that your children might have a hard time seeing your point of view because when stress levels are high, it's difficult to see things as they really are.

BEWARE AND BE AWARE OF BURNOUT

Have you ever seen a memorable TV commercial that was so good you even talked about it with your friends and family? One series of commercials I will never forget is an advertisement for Staples and their depiction of the "easy button." In each commercial, the answer to a crucial decision or crisis was resolved by a simple push of the big, red, "easy button."

In my experience with elite performers, I've learned that the "easy button" doesn't exist for those striving for excellence. If anything, the best of the best are more susceptible to pressing the "more challenging button." However, no matter how passionate your child is about reaching a goal or how much he loves what he's doing, he is susceptible to *burnout*.

Burnout is common and is not an indication of being mentally weak or that your child is doing something wrong, so rather than press the panic button, wondering if your son or daughter is experiencing burnout or not, let's talk about what burnout is and how to deal with it.

HOW DO I KNOW IF MY CHILD IS EXPERIENCING BURNOUT?

Just like you can sense yourself catching a cold, having the flu, or even falling in love, many characteristics indicate one may be experiencing burnout. As I have spoken with people who have experienced burnout, here's what they've said it's like:

- Feeling like you have unusually low energy and motivation for training

- Physical, mental, and emotional exhaustion

- Negative attitude toward practice and/or competition

- Feeling of lack of accomplishment

- Lack of enjoyment

This list does not include all potential indicators of burnout; however, if you're noticing that the demands of training and competition are beginning to be more stressful (negative stress) on your child rather than enjoyable, then be aware that he could *possibly* be experiencing burnout. How he responds could be the difference between experiencing optimal performance or deciding to call it quits.

WHAT BURNOUT IS NOT

Some of you may be worried because your child is experiencing each one of those distinguishing characteristics to a degree and feel that you should help him change something before it's too late. Before you do that, I want you to consider two more things.

First, a common stage performers go through is the plateau phase. This is when you just don't have the "umph" (for lack of a better word) you once had. You may have hit a plateau if training feels tedious and monotonous. This is *not* burnout. The plateau phase is temporary and doesn't necessarily lead to burnout. When the plateau phase sets in, people often overcome it by increasing focus.

Second, be aware of overtraining. Just like the plateau phase, this is *not* necessarily burnout. In any kind of performance training, over*loading* (deliberately making a drill faster, more difficult, heavier, and so on) is a beneficial training technique to increase performance and stamina; however, over*training* (practicing for too long) has an adverse effect on your performance, and prolonged overtraining can definitely lead to burnout. Going that extra mile may not be what's best for your child.

WHY DOES MY CHILD EXPERIENCE BURNOUT?

While other people can contribute to you experiencing burnout, most of the susceptibility factors are self-inflicted. Here are some reasons your child might experience burnout:

- Feeling of *having to* train, compete, eat right, and so on.

- Feeling obligated to do something for another person. If a child thinks this, his sense of autonomy is decreased, and his motivation is negatively affected.

- Sets unrealistic goals and expectations.

- Overly concerned about setbacks, mistakes, and not being "good enough."

- Defining self–worth by performance.

Once again, while this is not an extensive list of every reason youth experience burnout, these are a few of the main causes and may be the vine from which others stem.

HOW DO I HELP MY CHILD OVERCOME/AVOID BURNOUT?

Something to consider about burnout is that your child could use the same strategies to both avoid burnout and overcome it. Here are a few suggestions (the last list, I promise):

- Revisit original reasons for playing their sport.

- Rest. Rest. Rest.

- Make sure practice and competitions aren't all–consuming.

- Focus on quality of practice and not quantity.

- Mix it up! Put some variety into every day. Even a seemingly simple variation to a daily schedule can make a big difference.

Burnout should not be something your child focuses on avoid–ing; it's simply something to be aware of.

Activity: With your child, make a list of things he likes to do for fun. Take a look at that list and identify how often he is doing those things. To help recharge your child's mental batteries, make sure he is doing at least one thing he loves to do every day. His "time-out" activity doesn't have to occupy much time; its only purpose is to help him relax.

BREATHE ON PURPOSE

I was working with a young golfer, and as we were developing a game plan for an upcoming tournament, his mission was simple: Breathe better. While your child can do many things to remain cool under pressure, the universal mental skill every young athlete should learn is to breathe on purpose and with purpose. This is also called *deliberate breathing.*

When your child is feeling stressed, overwhelmed, and as if his mind is going a hundred miles per hour, chances are he's not breathing correctly, and, in sports, inconsistent breathing leads to poor performance. When your child neglects to breathe slowly and deeply, it can lead to a troublesome combination of muscle tension and narrowed attention, causing him to miss important information.

Helping your child bring attention to *his breath* will help enhance a sense of calm because he's bringing his attention to the most important moment of performance—the here and now. As your child learns how to master his breathing, this will reduce stress, increase energy levels, and reduce blood pressure. These benefits may not be enticing to your child, but all he needs to know is that as he learns to breathe deliberately, it will help him feel more relaxed, which can transfer to optimal performance.

If your son or daughter struggles with performance anxiety, gets heated when things don't go his or her way, or is in a high–pressure situation, train him or her to slow down and breathe. Just like all the other mental skills, the key is going to be to practice. Remember, when things get difficult and when the pressure is turned up, take time to breathe.

Activity: Have your child practice deliberate breathing by using a slow, deliberate breathing cadence of inhaling for five counts and then exhaling for five counts (the better he gets, the longer the inhale and exhale are). Make sure he isn't breathing into his shoulders and chest—his belly should be the only thing moving. Make sure he focuses on each individual breath. Invite him to scan his body for tense muscle groups and, on every exhale, say the word "relax" in his mind to loosen those muscles. If ineffective thoughts enter your child's mind, tell him to say, "let go" and return his focus to the present breath. This signifies to the mind that in this moment, your child is not going to let these thoughts have power over him. Do this exercise for 3–5 minutes per day.

I want you to pay attention to your breath. Take a long, deep inhale and a long, deep exhale. Bring your attention to your breathing, and as you begin to feel the tension in your body, relax it. A lot of times we hold tension in our necks, shoulders, and upper back. Let those muscles go. As you are able to relax your muscles and your body, you will be able to relax your mind and think a lot clearer. Another thing you can do is visualize. If you can picture a person, time, or place that brings you feelings of gratitude and joy, that will help you relax as well. As you practice this and do this, you will find yourself able to develop the ability to relax when you need it most. That would be in times of high stress levels.

TEACH YOUR CHILD
HOW TO FAIL

I WAS STANDING AT THE FRONT DESK OF AN ORGANI-
zation in San Antonio, Texas, and after I told the receptionist
what I do for a living, she sweetly asked, "Can you give me some
advice on how to help my son perform better?" This is a difficult
question to answer because to be accurate, it requires that I do a
number of follow—up questions: however, in some cases (like this
one in particular), I don't have that time. Rather than saying, "It
depends," I choose to give this response: "Teach your child how to
fail."

Someone once told me that the former coach of the Utah Jazz
Jerry Sloan said, "Good NBA players love to win, but Hall of Famers
hate to lose." I find that to be true with many of the performers I
work with, but let me be clear: even though high—level performers
hate to lose, they are so good because they know *how to lose*, and if
your child is going to be successful in sports, school, and life, this
is one of the most important mental skills she is going to need to
develop. You've probably heard Rocky's famous monologue in the
movie *Rocky Balboa*:

> Let me tell you something you already know. The world ain't all sun-
> shine and rainbows. It's a very mean and nasty place, and I don't care

how tough you are. It will beat you to your knees and keep you there permanently if you let it. You, me, or nobody is gonna hit as hard as life. But it ain't about how hard you hit. It's about how hard you can get hit and keep moving forward; how much you can take and keep moving forward. That's how winning is done! Now, if you know what you're worth, then go out and get what you're worth. But you gotta be willing to take the hits, and not pointing fingers saying you ain't where you wanna be because of him, or her, or anybody. Cowards do that and that ain't you. You're better than that![1]

THE BULLDOG STORY

One hot day a bull–herder was moving some bulls from one city to another. Everything was going smoothly until one of the bulls decided that he wanted to lie down and rest. With the rest of the herd moving forward, the young bull–herder knew that he couldn't let this bull stall. After offering a few encouraging words of, "C'mon, boy, let's keep going," coupled with a few gentle jabs to the bull's side with his stick, the bull's mind was made up—he wasn't going anywhere.

Without hesitation, the bull–herder turns to his trusted friend for help, his bulldog. Not only did this well–trained animal look like a ball of muscle with legs, but he also had the mentality to go with it. He walked right up to the bull, who was lying comfortably on the ground with no intentions to move, and got right in his face. This little bulldog was oblivious to the fact that he was outweighed and outmatched by this bull that was four times his size. After having no luck getting the bull to continue walking by nudging it with his nose, he began to bark, "You better get up! You better get up or you'll be in trouble!" (I don't speak bulldog, but I imagine this is what he was trying to convey to the bull.) Evidently the bull didn't speak bulldog either because he didn't move a muscle; that's when the bulldog jumped up and crushed the bull's nose!

Experiencing excruciating pain, the bull rose to its feet with the bulldog now dangling from his face. In an attempt to relieve itself from the grip of this small but powerful dog, the bull whipped the bulldog around like a ragdoll, slamming it on the ground over and over again. This little bulldog took a huge beating but never let go until the bull finally had enough and fell to the ground again. Realizing the bull had given up, the bulldog let go of the bull's nose and started to bark again: "You better get up or we're doing that again!" Now the bull speaks bulldog, so he gets up and hustles to join the rest of the herd.

To experience success, your child must learn how to develop the "bulldog mentality," the ability to take a hit and keep going strong. The question is how do you do that? In this chapter, I present four tools to help your child optimize those moments of defeat.

DEVELOP A PLAN

I'll never forget walking into the home of a young sixth-grade baseball player to do a mental training session. Before we started, I said, "Today, I'm going to teach you how to strike out." To which he quickly shot back, "Coach Su'a, I already know how to do that." Touché.

He was your typical great athlete who mentally struggled when things went bad, but rather than continue to let his reaction happen, he decided to choose his response to the ego-crushing and sometimes embarrassing strikeout. For the next forty-five minutes, we created a *Strikeout Routine*, and he decided what he was going to say to himself, how he was going to walk to the dugout, how he would take off his gloves, and even how his demeanor would be the rest of the game. This strategy served this young man well, and he was able to arm himself against failure by having a plan for when it happened rather than allowing it to disable him emotionally.

PREPARE TODAY FOR TOMORROW'S ADVERSITY

I'm not implying that you teach your child to adopt the doom-and-gloom mentality; I'm suggesting that the reason your child may struggle when tough times hit is not because she is mentally weak but rather because she doesn't have a plan for *when* it strikes.

One way to help your son or daughter plan ahead is a simple strategy called an "if-then" statement. Like my young baseball player mentioned, all he needed was a concrete idea of what he was going to do when things didn't go his way. When trouble looms, we begin to *catastrophize*, which is a cool psychological term that means to make something bigger than it really is. When we catastrophize, we lose a sense of control, and, as you know, once we feel we have lost a sense of control, we feel more anxiety, less motivation, and perhaps helplessness and hopelessness—not the ideal situation for optimal performance. Creating if–then statements helps put you (or your child) back in the driver's seat and helps you feel like you are in control and are acting rather than being acted upon.

When I teach my young adult students how to develop these statements, I invite them to write down everything that causes frustration in their respective performance. After they have their laundry list of possible performance distractions, I invite them to discuss how they are affected by these things. "It makes me mad," "I get depressed," or "It makes me want to give up" are common responses. It's always exciting for me to see the looks on their faces when I tell them it doesn't have to be that way.

When I tell them that they can choose their response to adversity before it actually happens, you can see the lightbulb go off in their minds. I challenge them to write down what they are going to *do, think, remember,* or *say* when they experience these hardships. Here are a few examples some of my students have come up with:

- *If* I don't want to go to practice, *then* I'm going to remind myself of my dream of playing in college.

- *If* my coach yells at me, *then* I'm going to focus on *what* he says and not *how* he's saying it.

- *If* I'm feeling really nervous before my performance, *then* I'm going to take three deliberate breaths.

Activity: Have your child write down a list of things that she would consider an obstacle. Ask her how these things currently affect her. After you discuss these things, have her write down effective "if-then" statements to give her the ability to remain in control when things don't go her way.

CHANGE THE WAY THEY FRAME FAILURE

Does this sound familiar? It should. You read about this when I wrote about teaching your children how to flex their optimistic muscles, and we revisited it when you learned about helping your child develop the right mind–set. Now I'm going to show you how this mental strategy can help your child learn how to fail well.

One of the best stories I've heard when it comes to effectively framing failure is that of Sarah Blakely, the founder of Spanx. This powerful CEO and billionaire knows a thing or two about success, but it was her father's advice on how to fail that helped her succeed at a young age, teaching her to "fail big." After school each day her dad would ask her, "So, what did you fail at today?" If she had no failures to report, he would be disappointed. She carried her father's council with her into her early entrepreneurial years when she could get no financial backing, no patent lawyer to support her, and no hosiery mill to produce her product. Remembering the lessons she received as a little girl helped Blakely develop something special— the ability to learn from failure. The more your child is able to learn from failure, the less she will fear it. One of the best ways to reframe failure is to ask yourself two questions: (1) what's the bright side of this situation? And (2) what did I learn from this failure?

"WHAT'S THE BRIGHT SIDE OF THIS SITUATION?"

When your child fails, it's easy to be negative. If you want your child to develop mental toughness, teach her how to identify what went well in *every* performance (even the poor ones). It's unhealthy to solely focus on the negative aspects of what just happened because when she replays his performance in her mind, she's going to use those memories to beat herself up, which will undermine her con– fidence for next time.

Activity: Identify the last time your child failed. Discuss with her the bright side of that failure. Did anything good happen in that situation? As parents we can sometimes focus too much on what our child needs to do to get better that she only develops an eye for what's wrong, without considering what went right.

"WHAT DID I LEARN FROM THIS FAILURE?"

Could you imagine your child sitting through a boring class that was going to be helpful for an upcoming test, and at the end of instruction she realizes that rather than take notes, all she did was complain about how she didn't want to be there? That's like failing in a performance and not learning the lesson! Failure is an opportunity to learn, and if your child is not learning the lessons, then that horrible experience she just went through might repeat itself sooner than later.

In 2013, America's Cinderella story in the NCAA Men's Division I Basketball Tournament was the Sweet Sixteen matchup between fifteenth–seeded Florida Gulf Coast University and third–seeded University of Florida. Thousands jumped on FGCU's underdog bandwagon; however, when the game ended, Florida won 62–50. During the press conference after the game, FGCU point guard Brett Comer told the world what he *learned* from this experience: "We learned that we can play with anyone in the nation. We learned that we can literally do anything that we put our minds to if we play with the right energy. We did some things here that will never be forgotten." Failures are lessons to be learned.

Activity: Discuss with your child lessons she learned from her recent failures and what she plans to do about it. Feel free to share a few failures of your own!

KEEP THINGS IN PERSPECTIVE

I was sitting at the kitchen table with one of my students, and she was describing to me how a recent failure was keeping her from progressing. When she was done, I asked her to grab something she considered to be small. She looked around the kitchen and grabbed a pen cap sitting in front of her. I asked, "Why did you choose that?" "Because it's the smallest thing I can see right now," she replied. I asked if someone were to walk into this house, what are the chances they would notice that pen cap immediately. She chuckled and said, "Not very likely." I asked her to hold that small pen cap right in front of her dominant eye. "Now how big is that 'small' object?" "It's not allowing me to see anything else," she replied. When our shortcomings and failures become the focus of our performance, that's all we see. Help your child not to fall into this trap by helping her keep things in perspective.

STREAKS AND SLUMPS

One day a dancer I work with called to tell me how she just gave the worst performance of her life—she was devastated. I asked her to do me a favor. I said, "Go grab a piece of paper, and let's document how you feel right now." She filled the page with rock-bottom emotions and painful thoughts. When we finished our conversation, I invited her to save that sheet of paper. When she asked why, I said that I would tell her later. Three months went by, and she called again. This time, however, words couldn't express how pumped she was after just finishing the performance of a lifetime! I smiled as she described the exhilaration of the moment, and, when she finished, I asked her to grab and read that sheet of paper I told her to save. She was amazed on what a difference three months made. The principle here is, *Slumps are temporary, so don't hit the panic button, and hot streaks are temporary, so don't be satisfied.* When adversity strikes, your child is going to have a difficult time keeping things in perspective. Make sure you as the parent are able to do so. Help your child realize that her performance is something she *does* and doesn't define who she *is*. As you continue to help your children enhance performance, do them a favor and teach them how to fail in the process.

Activity: When your child has a poor performance, have her capture everything in writing. How does she feel? What is she thinking? What is she doing wrong? Don't correct her; just let her speak. Save these answers because in the moment it's hard for her to realize that it's not the end of the world! The next time she has a stellar performance, pull out that sheet and have a good laugh reviewing what she wrote.

THE GIFT OF ATTENTION

It happens to the best of us—that moment when you are performing a task or in conversation with someone and your body is there, but your mind is somewhere else. In sports, this happens when your child is getting ready for a penalty kick but can't stop thinking, *What if I miss?* or it occurs when you're golfing and become annoyed by those loud people playing behind you. It can also happen to you at home, sitting at the dinner table with your family and trying to enjoy some time together, but your mind keeps drifting back to what happened earlier that day at work or a deadline you don't know if you'll be able to make. In all of these cases, a particular adjustment should be made to make that moment more enjoyable and help you perform at a higher level. A person must adjust his or her attention.

During one of my consultations, I shared with a student an analogy comparing our attention to a gift. Attention, like a gift, is something you give, and who or what your child gives her attention to will affect how she feels and ultimately performs.

Bouncing back from failure means helping your child refuse to allow anyone to *take* that gift from her. Developing the ability to purposefully *give* her the gift of attention to whomever and whatever she chooses is much more difficult during moments of perceived failure.

Activity: Ask your child what she should choose to think about and focus on and how she should choose to respond in a moment of adversity.

NOTE

1. *Rocky Balboa*, directed by S. Stallone (2006; United States: MGM Distribution).

[MENTAL SKILL #7]

TEACH YOUR CHILD HOW TO HAVE CONFIDENCE

SN'T IT INTERESTING HOW MANY PEOPLE HAVE ALL THE confidence in the world when they are younger, but as they grow older, they begin to analyze possible outcomes and care a little too much what other people think about them. Their confidence begins to shrink because of this, and their performance is adversely impacted.

I want you to imagine a confident person. How does this person carry him— or herself? What does this look like when this person walks into a room? How does this person speak? Chances are you are thinking about a specific person. When I think about the most confident people I know, I think of my children—Jarom (six), Mya (five), and Eliana (four).

When Jarom came home from kindergarten one day, my wife asked him, "What did you learn today, son?" He nonchalantly replied, "I didn't learn; I taught." Obviously intrigued with this answer, my wife continued her inquiry. "What do you mean you taught?" He said, "The teacher asked if anyone can sing 'Happy Birthday' in Spanish, so I taught the class how to do it." Melissa paused for a moment and reminded our son that he doesn't know how to speak Spanish. I told Melissa that there was probably some kid in that class who really does speak Spanish but was questioning himself because Jarom owned it.

Mya is fearless when it comes to swimming. When we were on vacation one summer, we were in the pool, and we heard Mya shout, "One, two, three, go! Just do it!" She would then put her head in the water and start swimming. The other two kids watched her in amazement as they witnessed their sister teach herself how to swim.

One day Melissa was at a car dealership with the three kids, when our youngest daughter, Eliana, walked up to a man cleaning the floors and said, "Hey, I like your muscles!" Melissa hustled to grab little Eli's hand and walked away before she blurted anything else on her mind. "Sweetheart, you don't say that to strangers." "What, Mama? He has nice muscles." Kids are fearless sometimes.

Many of the youth I work with have the physical prowess to perform at a high level, but it's their lack of confidence that gets in their way. This might be the case with your child. Maybe he had a poor performance a long time ago and keeps hitting the repeat button in his mind—not to learn from his mistakes, but to put himself down. This chapter is aimed to help you help your children minimize their tendency to be bullied by their own thoughts.

HELP YOUR CHILD MASTER SELF-TALK

Teach your sons and daughters that they are the most influential people they speak to every day. What they say to themselves will affect their emotions, which will have an impact on how their bodies feel and the effort they give, which will ultimately influence their performance. Then, based on how they interpret the outcome of the performance, it's likely to reinforce their initial thoughts.

What your children say to themselves has a tremendous impact on their confidence, and while they cannot control everything that happens to them, if they develop the mental skill of mastering their internal dialogue, it will serve them well in every aspect of their lives.

WHY IT WORKS

Imagine having an empty ten-ounce cup in one hand and a

pitcher with a gallon of water in the other hand. Now if I were to tell you to *completely empty* the water in the pitcher into the cup, how much water would be in the cup? I hope you said, "Ten ounces." My next question would be, "Why only ten ounces when you poured the entire gallon of water into it?" Your answer will be, "Because that's how much the cup holds." My final question is, "Then where is the rest of the water?" To which you would answer, "All over the floor."

All of us give mental real estate to the things we choose to give our attention to. Note that although our minds are powerful, our consciousness has limited capacity, which means there is only so much we can possibly focus on. Like trying to dump a gallon of water into a ten-ounce cup, it doesn't matter how many things you *want* to focus on, the reality is there's only so much space. This matters because the things we allow to occupy our minds, or fill our cup, can help us or damage our performance. Teach your children to fill their cup, by choosing what to say to themselves.

THE POWER OF NEGATIVE SELF-TALK

I was talking to a friend of mine who told me of an experience he had during an Ironman Triathlon he participated in. He said that at one point of the race he found himself cycling beside a strong triathlete. They were neck and neck zooming through the course, neither willing to relinquish the lead. At a certain point, they had to ascend a steep hill against a powerful headwind. As they battled against this brutal climb, the man my friend was competing against exclaimed, "I hate this wind." This declaration of mental fatigue gave my friend a boost of confidence, and he quietly responded, "See ya!" bolting past him, never to see him again during the race.

Phrases like, "I'm terrible!" "I have the worst luck," "I just got lucky," "It's just no use," "I hate this!" and "I'll never be able to . . ." are all examples of negative self-talk and are psychological weapons your child uses against himself to sabotage his ability to succeed. Many people think these innocent sayings don't have much of an impact, but what they say in their minds does matter, no matter how innocent it may appear.

If anyone should be your child's number-one fan, it should be him! He should be cheering himself on and feeding his mind with encouragement more than anyone else. Having support from coaches, parents, and friends is a bonus. And if your child is not getting the support he needs from these people, he need not worry; he has himself—and what your child says to and about himself has a tremendous impact on performance.

FILL YOUR CUP WITH A PERSONAL SLOGAN

Let's play a game. It's called "Name That Slogan." Currently, what's the McDonald's slogan? How about Kellogg's Frosted Flakes? Finally, do you know Nike's slogan? If you said, "I'm Lovin' It," "They're Grrreat!" and "Just Do It," then you're correct. So what does this have to do with confidence? Let me show you.

One day I was in a training with a group of military servicemen and women, when the instructor asked, "Do any of you have a quote or saying you say to yourself when things are difficult?" A soldier raised his hand and shared with the class what he says to himself. The instructor was intrigued, so he asked, "What does that mean?" He related that when he was young in his military career, he had a bad habit of complaining too much. One day a leader pulled him aside and asked him what the "maximum effective range" was for numerous weapons. Confused, yet prepared, this soldier accurately answered each question. Finally, his leader asked, "What's the maximum effective range of your complaining?" When he had no answer, his leader helped him out: "Zero meters. It's never effective to complain." From that point on, "Zero meters" became that soldier's personal slogan.

Your child's personal slogan is a phrase he chooses to live by or focus on that triggers a certain emotion or behavior. When he chooses to fill up his cup with his slogan, it's going to trigger a certain emotion or behavior. His slogan needs to be powerful, meaningful, and something that will help him focus on the possibilities and not the probabilities of a situation. If the statement doesn't mean anything to your child, then it's going to be hard for him to use it as an effective tool when he needs it most. This happened to my daughter Eliana.

It's amazing how children can be raised in the same house, eat the same food, receive the same teachings, and have the same parents but be completely different! For example, as parents know, discipline must be administered with love but will affect each child differently. There was a time when our four-year-old, Eliana, couldn't stand going to "time-out." She would do *anything* to not have to sit still for a given amount of time. On one particular day, she did something inappropriate and was subsequently sent to time-out. She pleaded not to go, but a consequence had to be served. She stomped to the dreaded corner and began to cry. After being there for about sixty seconds, our daughter was beginning to calm down, and she was saying something to herself. My wife and I quietly tiptoed closer to hear what she was saying: "I'm okay. I'm okay. I'm okay . . ." Melissa and I looked at each other and were very impressed, but before we could express our thoughts with Eli, her willpower was drained, and she yelled out, "I'm *not* okay!" which induced a waterfall of tears streaming down her cheeks.

Mantras and positive affirmations are inherently beneficial, but if they are empty words that lack personal meaning and conviction, they won't adequately trigger the powerful positive emotions your child needs at that moment. In our little Eliana's case, simply saying "I'm okay" wasn't personal or powerful enough to bring her out of her slump.

Your child's personal slogan doesn't have to be words; it can be the thought of a person, a good memory, or the thought of winning the championship or getting a good grade on the test. It doesn't matter what the slogan is, the purpose is for your child to *fill his cup*, or, in other words, choose where to give his focus rather than let it happen. When your child decides to occupy his mind with what he wants to happen and what he's going to do about it, an interesting thing occurs. Those ineffective thoughts that had the tendency to fill his mind have less of an impact—not because they don't exist, but because there's less room for them to slide in. I'll be the first to say that effective self-talk isn't going to "cure" negative thinking. We're human, so of course ineffective thoughts are going to enter our minds. But you can teach your child to deliberately train the way he thinks by developing a powerful personal slogan.

Activity: Help your child develop a short and powerful personal slogan. Some of my students have used phrases like "I got this!" or "I'm a beast!" or "I own this!" or "Suck it up, princess!" Identify situations in which your child would use it, and challenge him to write it down and put it in a place he will constantly see it.

Note: Children's self-talk tends to be the words their parents say to them, so don't worry if they may sound a bit aggressive—it may be what's helpful for their particular performance.

YOUR CHILD'S CONFIDENCE IS STRENGTHENED WHEN HE STRENGTHENS HIS ABILITY TO VISUALIZE SUCCESS

It's 2:00 a.m. and a shriek comes from the room of a three-year-old. Imagine the parents running to rescue their child to realize he is having a nightmare. He's lying in his little bed, wiggling back and forth; his heart is racing; breathing is heavy; and he's crying, sweating, and screaming. All of a sudden, the child pops up, opens his eyes, and quickly realizes that it was just a dream.

Small children aren't the only ones who are awakened by bad dreams; it happens to all of us. I want to bring your attention to an interesting phenomenon that occurs when we have a vivid dream (good or bad). Like the child in this story, even though the events taking place were a figment of his imagination, his body responded as if it were really happening. This is an important principle to understand. Your child might be lacking confidence because what he sees in his mind is creating tremendous anxiety, fear, and doubt. Like all of the other mental skills, learning to visualize success is a skill that can be taught.

THE POWER OF IMAGERY

Imagery is an important tool many high-level performers use. I was sitting on a plane once next to a world-renowned surgeon headed to Austin, Texas, to speak about a surgical procedure he invented. We started talking, and he asked me to show him how I train people. When I talked about imagery, he was intrigued. He shared with me that he didn't realize it but he uses imagery before every operation. "Justin, every time I do a surgery, the patient's life is in my hands. Before I operate, I go to a quiet room and perform the operation flawlessly in my mind." I congratulated him on the effective use of this mental skill, and he was excited to learn that Olympic athletes do the same thing before they perform.

The problem is that youth might be using imagery to undermine their confidence rather than strengthen it. Teaching your child how to paint a vivid and controllable picture in his mind can help him have the confidence to execute a performance before he actually has to do it. Not only is it important to learn *how* to visualize effectively but also *what* to visualize.

PAINTING THE BEST PICTURE POSSIBLE

Imagery is the ability to create or re-create an experience in your mind. The best way to practice is to deliberately remember a past experience. It can be when you got married, the birth of your child, or what you did yesterday; the key is to get that picture in your head. To make that picture even more powerful, include all five of your senses (sight, sound, smell, touch, and taste). The more senses you include, the more effective this technique will be.

I used this technique once with a baseball player I was working with. He called me and explained that he was in the worst slump of his life. The first question I asked was, "Can you remember the last time you were on fire?" He thought about it for a while and said, "Yes, I can." I asked him to take me there. "Who were you playing against? What color were your uniforms? Was it day or night? How many fans were there?" By forcing him to answer my questions, I was making the picture in his mind stronger, thus increasing its influence on his confidence.

Activity: Help your child build his confidence by asking him to revisit successful moments in his mind. Ask him questions that will cause him to search his memories for details, which will impact the vividness of the image.

IT'S NOT BAD TO SEE THE BAD

Confident people aren't afraid to face challenges, while people who lack confidence don't want to consider that something bad might happen. One way to enhance confidence is to accomplish goals, and to help with that, let me introduce you to next principle, called *mental contrasting.*[1] It involves creating a contrast in our minds between the positive and negative aspects on our journey to goal achievement. It involves identifying a goal that you want to achieve, then for thirty seconds visualizing all of the positive aspects of attaining that goal; when those thirty seconds are up, visualize all of the challenges and obstacles you will face to attain that goal; then switch back to the positive aspects, then the adversity and so on. The research shows that this skill increases the likelihood that an individual will achieve his or her goals and enhance confidence.

THE NERVOUS STUDENT

I worked with a teenager who was very talented. She was articulate, a great athlete, and one of those people you know will be successful in whatever she does. The only problem was that she wanted to do so well on the SAT and ACT that she began to create too much anxiety for herself. Just thinking about taking these standardized tests raised her heart rate and made her nervous, so mental contrasting was just what we did. Every day I saw her, we would do a three-minute session of mental contrasting. I had her envision walking into the test confidently, in control, and successfully answering the questions. Then I had her imagine herself running into a question she didn't know, having a proctor who wasn't nice, being the last one to finish, and so on. When the test day arrived, she let me know, she had a lot more confidence because she saw herself respond to the adversity before it actually happened. Teach your child that it's not bad to see the bad that might happen; however, make sure he contrasts it with the good.

Activity: For two minutes and thirty seconds, strengthen your child's confidence by having him visualize success for thirty seconds and what it will take. Then for the next thirty seconds, tell him to see the hardship he will experience. Then move back to the successful images. Finish when he has visualized the good for three rounds and the bad for two.

SOME MORE IMAGERY TIPS

If your child isn't used to doing imagery or doesn't feel he can control the pictures in his mind, don't worry. This comes with prac-tice, and, worst—case scenario, you don't use this skill with him. I would like to share with you a few more imagery tips that will prove beneficial to help build a picture to help your child develop and sustain confidence.

INSIDE VERSUS OUTSIDE

I want you to imagine yourself doing three push—ups. When you did those push—ups in your mind, did you watch yourself do them (third—person view), or did you imagine as if you were really doing them (first—person view)? Research shows that both perspectives have their benefits. Outside imagery (external) tends to help with mechanic correction and confidence building, while inside imagery (internal) elicits more muscle activity. So which one is better? Nei-ther is better than the other.

REPETITION

Your child's body can only be pushed so far, and he can only get a limited amount of physical reps in. However, with effective imag-ery, he can do mental reps that will prove beneficial. Some studies have shown that imagery—trained athletes who can imagine their per—formance will actually have a physiological response to the pictures they see in their minds (just like the three—year—old nightmare story). Instead of just playing a highlight reel in his head, invite your child to imagine specific movements and techniques over and over again.

SEE THE PROCESS

Your child is going to have the tendency to just imagine win—ning the game, getting the A, or making the team. This is good, but to make it even better, teach him to also visualize the specific things he is going to need to do to get there. It would be helpful to have him visualize himself running sprints at practice, practicing the piano, writing that paper, or getting up early to go for a run before school. He makes himself more likely to do these things if he sees it in his mind first.

Confidence is a feeling your child has in a given moment, and it can be built in many different ways. Teaching him to master his self—talk and how to see success before it happens are powerful skills to facilitate confidence growth. However, the number—one way to build it is simply to get out there and work.

NOTE

1. G. Oettingen, M. Wittchen, and P. M. Gollwitzer, "Regu—lating Goal Pursuit through Mental Contrasting with Implemen—tation Intentions," In E. A. Locke and G. P. Latham, eds., *New Developments in Goal Setting and Task Performance* (New York: Rout—ledge, 2013), 523–548.

TEACH YOUR CHILD
HOW TO BE A LEADER

I'S SAD TO SEE COLLEGE COACHES THROWING basketballs at players, parents yelling at their kids in the middle of the game, and once-revered athletes falling to performance-enhancing drugs or making bad decisions in their personal lives. And while all this is happening, our children are watching, processing, and learning.

The time has come to train our children to be leaders, but unfortunately we often tell them what to do without teaching them how to do it. I've been blessed to have had parents, coaches, teachers, and others I look up to who have shown me good examples on how to lead others. Here are four principles to remember to help you teach your child how to lead.

HELP YOUR CHILD TO UNDERSTAND
THAT LEADERS SERVE OTHERS

I was ten years old, and the big day had arrived. It was the Mustang Championship game between my team and our archrivals, the Marlins. The game was scheduled to start in the late morning, and we usually arrived to the field an hour before the game to begin stretching and our pregame routine, but this day was different. My dad was the head coach and told me that we would be arriving at the ballpark extra early so he could work with another player before the game. On our way to the game, I kept thinking about how good it's going to be for my dad to give a player some extra coaching before everyone showed up. We were going to need everyone to bring their A-game if we were going to beat the competition. As we approached the field, a car was already parked by the dugout, but I didn't recognize whose car it was. As my father and I walked to the field, I saw Wayne Venaski, the star player for the Marlins, sitting in one of the dugouts with his dad. "Hey, Wayne!" my father shouted. Wayne and his father stood and came out to meet us. His dad expressed gratitude to my father for taking the time to go over some pitching fundamentals before he pitched against us in the championship game.

I couldn't believe it! My father, the head coach for our team, was helping the best player for the *other* team! I childishly thought, *Maybe he's going to teach him the wrong things so he'll mess up and we'll win.* That thought was quickly debunked when I heard him using the same terminology and fundamentals he used with me. After a short but helpful coaching session with Wayne and his dad, they exchanged hugs, and we each went back to our respective dugouts.

About an hour later, the field was packed with parents, friends, and other players supporting two great teams vying for the championship trophy. It was a great contest. Wayne pitched against us and did an outstanding job. When the final out was made, we were victorious; however, I don't remember the score, how I did that game, or any highlights in particular. The one thing I'll never forget was how my Dad taught me the valuable lesson that *people are more important than things, including victory.*

THE BEST LEADERS LEAD FROM THE FRONT

As parents, help your child understand that whether she has the title "team captain" or not, she can still be a leader. She should expect to be a leader. Unfortunately, the youngsters today are exposed to bad examples when it comes to leadership. "Do as I say, not as I do" is a common message that is being sent to the rising generation, and it is evident by the way team captains are treating those who follow.

I attended high school in California, and during that time, we were known for having an outstanding baseball team. As a young player, I noticed something interesting about the team captains my freshman and sophomore years. Rather than make the underclass-men pick up all the equipment and prep the field, they did it. When practice was over, and the sun was beginning to set, I can remember seeing the team captain, who happened to be leading the team in every offensive category those years, the only one left watering the field. When it came time for me to serve my team as their captain, I followed the example of those who showed me the way—not because they told me to do it, but because they actually did it.

Teach your child not to complain when everyone else is, to hustle even more when her team is losing, to keep her eyes open for a teammate in need, and to keep her head up when she makes a mistake.

MIRROR VERSUS MAGNIFYING GLASS APPROACH

I once took a teacher improvement class, and our final consisted of everyone inviting a guest to attend the last day of class to watch each other teach a fifteen-minute mini lesson. When it was my turn, I was more excited than nervous because teaching is what I love to do, and I feel pretty confident doing so. For weeks I worked on my lesson plan and perfectly constructed the lesson flow, mastered the delivery of each story I would share, and made sure to punctuate the memorable sound bites.

The fifteen minutes flew by because I was in the zone. I knocked it out of the park! When I sat down, Melissa, who was my guest, clenched her fist, signaling a confirmation that I just nailed it. When the instructor passed out the grades, I noticed a lot of A's and B's, and I felt I was going to get one of the highest grades in the class. When I saw my grade I was shocked—a B–. I needed an explanation, so I walked right into the instructor's office after class and asked him why I deserved such a low grade.

Rather than give me details about my actual performance, he

started with an analogy, "Justin, when you hold a mirror up to your face, what do you see?" Although I had no idea where he was going with this, I answered, "Myself." He followed up with another question: "Now, if you grab a magnifying glass and hold that up to your face, what are you going to see?" Another question I knew the answer to. "Whatever you are holding it up to will be bigger," I replied. "Justin," he continued, "there are two types of teachers: *mirror* approach teachers and *magnifying glass* approach teachers." He explained: "The *mirror* approach teacher is more concerned about themselves: 'What am *I* going to say?'; 'What stories am *I* going to share?'; and 'What are they going to think about *me*?' The *magnifying glass* approach teacher sees teaching completely differently: 'What questions am I going to ask to help *the students* discover the answer?'; 'What stories am I going to ask *them* to share?'; and 'What can I do to make it better for the *students*?'" Then my instructor said the phrase I'll never forget: "Justin, you're a mirror approach teacher, but once you learn how to be a magnifying approach teacher, you'll have more of an impact." Those words changed my view on teaching, coaching, parenting, and leadership. Teach your child to strengthen her capacity to lead by following the advice of a quote I once heard: "A leader does not think less of himself, but thinks about himself less."

Activity: Identify with your child what she can do to better serve her teammates, coaches, and others. This isn't to become the coach's pet, gain favor, or impress anyone; it's to create a culture of leaders.

TEACH YOUR CHILD TO CATCH OTHERS WINNING

By "catch others winning," I mean to look for people doing something good while no one else is watching. One of the best examples of this happened while I was a youngster on the pitcher's mound during a game. I can vividly remember having a runner on first base, and his lead to second was a little too big for my liking, so I threw the ball to Chris, the first baseman, to see if we could get that runner out. We were close but to no avail. Chris tossed the ball back to me, and the runner took another big lead. This time I decided to pitch the ball to Jordan, the catcher. After catching the ball, Jordan made a snap throw to Chris to catch the runner sleeping, but he was safe once again. All of a sudden, my father, and head coach, came out of the dugout yelling at the top of his lungs, "Great job, Joey! I see you, buddy! Great job!" Now, let's recap: I (Justin) threw the ball to Jordan, who then threw the ball to Chris—no Joey involved.

Before I explain what Joey did, let me tell you a little bit about him. He was one of the younger and therefore smaller guys on the team. He didn't hit, run, or field too well, and to protect him from getting hurt (especially at such a young age), it was best to put him in the outfield—deep right field.

In this particular instance, when Jordan threw the ball to Chris, Joey took two shuffles to his left—he was backing up the throw. In case the ball got past Chris, Joey was positioning himself to be there. Granted, the ball would have probably rolled past Joey as well, but that didn't matter; Joey had a responsibility and he did it. *It doesn't matter where you play, but how.* The principle I really want to emphasize is that it took a loving coach to catch Joey "winning" while no one was paying attention to what he was doing.

As your child develops the ability to pay attention and express effective praise to her teammates when they have a quiet victory, it will help others create winning streaks. By "effective praise," I mean to be specific and name the actual behavior they witnessed. In the case with Joey and my dad, Joey knew exactly what he did well, and it was no surprise to see Joey continue to back up the throw every time the catcher threw the ball to the first baseman.

GUESS WHO?

One of my favorite and most memorable practices I had as the head coach of my little 10U baseball team was when we did an activity called, "I'm Your #1 Fan!" It was early in the season, and our team chemistry was struggling. We didn't have any leaders, and the unity was next to zero. With these players being so young, it was my responsibility to teach them how to treat each other.

One practice I had each of their names written on a small strip of paper, and before our two–hour workout began, I had each of them draw a name from the pile. After each player had the name of one their teammates, I told them, "Okay, boys, the person you have in your hands is your favorite player on the team. You are his number–one fan. Throughout the entire practice, it's your job to encourage him, push him, challenge him, and help him." But there was a catch. At the end of the practice, each player had to guess who their number–one fan was, "Your job," I told them, "is to make as many people as possible think you are their number–one fan."

From the first drill, my players were encouraging each other, talking to each other during breaks, picking each other up when they messed up, and laughing a lot. I don't mean to get cheesy, but I actually got emotional witnessing an increase of love, enthusiasm, and leadership. When practice was over, I asked them if they noticed the difference, and the response was overwhelming. I did my best to convey to them that all we have is each other, and that if we are going to do great things, we need to treat each other with respect. On that day, I can honestly say that they learned what it meant to catch each other winning.

Activity: Invite your child to catch others winning at school, on her team, and especially at home. The key is to not only witness others winning, but to share it with that person. This helps your child develop leadership, builds the confidence in the other person, and strengthens the relationship between them. I also invite you as Mom or Dad to strive to catch your children winning.

TEACH YOUR CHILD
HOW TO CHANGE

O NE DAY A MAN CAME INTO MY OFFICE UNAN-
nounced. "Are you Justin?" he asked angrily. Deliberately smil—
ing, I answered in the affirmative. "Then let me tell you what's
happening," he continued. "I just got fired, I'm going through a
divorce, my kids can't stand me, I'm bankrupt, and I'm sleeping on
the living room floor of some guy I don't know." He paused for a
moment and said, "What's this [trash] you teach people?" Just so
you know, he didn't use the word *trash*. Before I answered his ques—
tion, I wasn't about to let him walk into my office and talk to me
like that. "First of all, who are you? And how did you find me?"

"[Greg] is my name, and my friend said that you might be able to
help me. So, tell me about this [trash] you teach." I told him that I am
a mental conditioning coach, and I use mental skills training to help
people enhance their ability to focus, develop routines, manage their
energy, and ultimately be more efficient and effective in whatever
they do. When I finished, he wasted no time to say, "That [trash]
won't work with me because I'm fifty years old, I've seen and done
things you couldn't even imagine, and you can't teach an old dog
new tricks." I didn't hesitate to say, "You're right." He was shocked.
"What?" he asked. "I said *you're right*, I can't teach you a thing if

your attitude is like that. We would be wasting our time if I tried to teach you with the mind–set you have right now—and I highly value my time." Now he was on the defensive, "Well, will it work?" I answered honestly, "I don't know." Now a bit confused, he asked, "You don't know?" I told him that having the best coach in the world doesn't guarantee championships, having the best teacher in the world doesn't guarantee straight A's, and having a mental conditioning coach doesn't guarantee mental toughness. However, having someone to teach you these things will put you in a better position to be successful. "Okay, I'll do it," he grumbled. "[Greg], I'm going to ask you to do things you've probably never done before. I'm going to ask you to think about things in a way that might be completely contrary to what you're used to. But I need you to be committed to do these things." Greg obliged, and we got to work.

After working together for about one month, Greg walked into my office unannounced again (he was good at doing that). I asked how he was doing, and he said, "Nothing has changed." He continued, "I'm still unemployed, the divorce is still pending, my kids aren't speaking to me, I have no money, now my car broke down, and I'm *still* sleeping on the living room floor of this guy's house—but the only good thing is, I know him a little better now." When he finished, I asked, "So you came in just to tell me that?" He smiled and said, "No. I came in to tell you that even though my situation hasn't changed, my mind–set has. I'm not devastated like I used to be. I'm doing something about it now." People can change.

Your child might get caught in the trap of thinking that he can't change, he's never going to be good at math, he's always going to ride the bench, he'll never be able to do what he wants. Teach him that these thoughts are wrong. Here are two principles to help your child change.

BE HUMBLE

If there was one thing I could go back and change in my life, I know exactly what it would be—a specific conversation I had with my father over the phone. I was in my junior year at BYU and was struggling on the mound. I didn't have the tenacity I had before, the velocity on my fastball was diminishing, and my breaking pitches weren't as sharp as they were in the years past.

Anytime I'm looking for help in any aspect of my life, I go to my heroes—my wife or my parents. In this particular instance, I was in desperate need of council and reached out to my dad. I told him what was going on, what I was doing, and what I believed I wasn't doing. Now here comes a not−so−shining moment in my life: After my father began to give me advice and council, I said two words that made me no longer teachable—"I know." By saying, "I know," I communicated to my dad that I could no longer be coached or learn more.

Years have passed since that simple yet memorable exchange, and the phrase "I know" has not left my lips since then. If someone is teaching me something, I'm willing to learn.

EMPTY YOUR CUP

I once heard a story about a man who went to visit a famous Zen master. The Zen master graciously invited the man into his home and offered him something to drink. The two sat at a table, and the Zen master poured a drink into the man's cup to the brim and then kept pouring. The man watched the overflowing cup and urgently exclaimed, "Stop! No more will go in!" "You are like this cup," the master replied. "How can I teach you unless you first empty your cup?"

Humility is a sign that your cup is not full and that you are ready to learn. If your child wants to change, he must understand that there is more to learn. The problem with our own children is that many of them are willing to learn, just not from Mom or Dad. I can't count how many times parents have come up to me saying that everything I told their child to do is *exactly* what they've been saying for years!

One way to help your child be more open to receive your feed−back is to be humble yourself. Acknowledging that you don't know it all as a parent and are willing to learn is helpful for your child to see. Allowing your child to teach *you* something, give *you* some council, and offer *his* opinion will help him see that even as adults, we still have things to learn. Now, I also understand that no matter

how humble you may be, or how willing you are to learn, sometimes no matter what you say as Mom or Dad, your child would
much rather hear it from someone else—and that's okay!

Activity: Finding the answers that affect change is sparked by
asking the right questions. Have your child come up with a list
of questions he can ask himself to serve as accountability for
the changes he needs to make.

For example, I have a golfer that asks himself five questions before each shot, (1) Am I relaxed? (2) Am I confident?
(3) Am I focused on this shot? (4) Am I breathing properly?
(5) Am I having fun? He's the one who came up with these
questions, and he's the one who answers them for himself.
Doing this helps him make the immediate adjustments necessary as opposed to letting negative momentum drag him down
from shot to shot. Humility is the key to change.

HAVE A GROWTH MIND-SET

Dr. Carol Dweck wrote a fantastic book called *Mindset: The
New Psychology of Success* that I highly recommend. Her research
is based on neuroplasticity, which means that our brains are like a
muscle and can grow as we continue to deliberately strengthen neu-
rological connections. So what does that mean? It's more evidence
that your child can change!

She talks about two different mind-sets: *fixed* and *growth*. The
reason your child might be struggling to change might not be because
he doesn't want to or lack the capacity to do so; it might be because
he doesn't know how. The *fixed* mind-set is one that believes your
skill level and habits are permanent and cannot be changed, while
the *growth* mind-set believes that just because you can't do something
now doesn't mean you'll never be able to do it. Dweck and her team
discovered that essentially five categories separate the *fixed* and *growth*
mind-set, and the reason it may be difficult for your child to change
could be because he is adopting the wrong mind-set.

FAILURE

If children have a *fixed* mind–set, failure is fatal. They hate to fail because they attach failure to their self–worth. To children with this mind–set, failure isn't something that happens; it defines who they are. When a person with a *fixed* mind–set fails, his or her confidence decreases and motivation drops. The *fixed* mind–set will leave your child less resilient because setbacks are so devastating that it will disable him emotionally.

With the *growth* mind–set, on the other hand, failure is *not* fatal but rather an opportunity to learn. People with this mind–set view failure as an event, but it doesn't define who they are. As a result of having this mind–set, they can bounce back a lot quicker.

CHALLENGES

A child with the *fixed* mind–set wants to stay far away from challenges. His interpretation of failure makes it difficult to accept a challenging task because there is a high probability that he may fail, which would be devastating. Children who have adopted the *fixed* mind–set are likely to procrastinate, make excuses, or try to sabotage themselves so they have a reason attached to why they failed.

Someone with the *growth* mind–set loves a challenge. Kids with this mind–set are focused on enjoying the journey. They completely understand they might fail, might get a little bloody, be a little sore, and get a little fatigued, but it's what they signed up for! Your son or daughter with the *growth* mind–set realizes that at the end of the journey, he or she is going to be different. The journey is going to stretch your child and make him stronger physically, emotionally, and spiritually. They love challenges because they don't fear failure.

EFFORT

When it comes to effort level, *fixed* mind–set children don't like to exert it. They feel that the more effort they give, the less competent they are. If an activity doesn't come easy, they would rather not do it. You can see the *fixed* mind–set youth from a mile away, because when he begins to lose, his effort level drops, which enables him to use the excuse, "I didn't do well because I didn't try that hard." Not trying is the ego—saving excuse for the *fixed* mind—set.

The *growth* mind—set in terms of effort level is completely different. This mind—set isn't affected by the score or the circumstance. It doesn't matter if your child is winning or losing; if people are watching or if he's alone, regardless of the situation, he's committed to give 100 percent. Giving his best effort is paramount because he knows that his best will gradually get better over time. Children with the *growth* mind—set understand that their best effort today will not be as good as their best in the future.

FEEDBACK

Kids with the *fixed* mind—set hate people telling them what to do, especially if they don't like the person giving the feedback. If they have to be corrected, it is detrimental to their self—worth; they don't feel they're good enough. The only feedback they like to receive is when people tell them how great they are. Negative feedback or constructive criticism isn't welcome because they don't feel like they can make the adjustments necessary to improve.

The individual with the *growth* mind—set is willing to soak up as much information as possible to get better. They don't get offended when a coach, teacher, or parent teaches them in a firm way. This doesn't mean they enjoy getting yelled at; it just means they pay attention to *what* the feedback is and not *how* it is being delivered (although how you deliver it is important). While those with the *growth* mind—set will freely take advice, this isn't to say they are necessarily people—pleasers. You don't have to listen to everyone to be considered a person with the *growth* mind—set.

SUCCESS OF OTHERS

Youth with the *fixed* mind—set feel less confident when someone else succeeds. They have the belief, "If someone else succeeds, that means I'm a failure." Additionally, to protect their ego the children with the *fixed* mind—set will claim that the other person "got lucky" or wasn't deserving of their achievement.

Your child with the *growth* mind—set views the success of others as encouragement to do better herself. Another's achievement makes him think, "If they can do it, so can I!" They are likely to ask the successful individual what *they* did to succeed and how to do the same.

SWITCHING FROM FIXED TO GROWTH

According to Dr. Dweck, the process is simple (but not easy). Help your child change by following this three—step formula: (1) Recognize fixed thoughts, (2) remember you have a choice to think what you want, and (3) replace fixed thoughts with growth thoughts.[1]

SO WHAT?

Pay close attention to your child's mind—set. He will reveal his mind—set in how he responds to failure, the amount of effort he decides to give when things aren't looking good, the desire he has to attack a challenge, how he responds to feedback, and, finally, what he says when someone else is successful.

Help your child understand that his mind—set is a decision he can make every day, and the mind—set he chooses to have when he leaves home every morning just might be one of the most important decisions he makes all day.

Activity: Sit down with your child (or have a meeting with your entire team if you're a coach) and discuss the *fixed* versus *growth* mind-set, and help your child (or team) understand the general difference between the two. Next, write down all of the categories (failure, challenges, effort, feedback, and suc-cess of others), and go through each one and ask the question, "What would be the thoughts a person with the fixed mind-set would have about [failure]? What would a person with the growth mind-set think?" You'll see your child's answers will be spot on. Also, as you're doing this activity, you'll help him discover that maybe he's had the fixed mind-set all along, but it's never been pointed out to him like this before.

NOTES

1. C. S. Dweck, *Mindset: The New Psychology of Success* (New York: Random House, 2006).

[MENTAL SKILL #10]

TEACH YOUR CHILD HOW TO ENJOY THE JOURNEY

I T WAS AUGUST 20, 2011, AND I FOUND MYSELF AT THE
starting line of the first and only marathon I'll ever run. If you
meet people who have completed a marathon, ask them why they
would go through such a grueling mental and physical task. You'll
hear explanations such as, "I did it for someone with an illness," "I
love to run," or "It's something I've always wanted to do." If you
ask me why I decided to run 26.2 miles, I'm going to be honest—I
was forced.

While that's not the complete truth, let me share with you how
I ended up running the Park City Marathon that year. Two weeks
previous to this particular summer morning, Melissa and I were celebrating seven years of marriage. She asked me if I would be inter-
ested in running a marathon with her, and, not thinking she was
actually serious (although I should have known she was), I naively
agreed to it. Imagine the shock I experienced when she told me that
the only marathon we would be able to do was going to take place
in two weeks—and that she already signed us up! This was crazy,
dangerous, and exciting at the same time. Melissa and I are avid
exercisers, and although we didn't necessarily "train" our bodies for
the journey ahead, we felt that we were in good enough shape to
give it a shot. Never doing that again.

Melissa and I are both competitive individuals, especially when we are competing against each other; however, we agreed that in this situation, all we wanted was to focus on is finishing together and enjoying the journey. For the next five hours, we battled heat, fatigue, and the pain of muscles we didn't even know existed, but we never stopped. Our focus of enjoying the journey protected us from having a bad attitude amid the adversity we experienced. To us, it didn't matter that we were being passed up by people twenty years our senior or ten years our junior. We weren't measuring our success on how we fared compared to others but on taking one more step toward to finish line. After tremendous patience, a little laughter, and lots of encouraging words to each other, we crossed the finish line together. (Let it be known that I actually finished a split–second before Melissa, but that's besides the point.)

When we look back on that crazy and fun accomplishment, the same lesson comes to mind: *You're a lot more likely to enjoy the journey when you decide to do so before the journey begins.* The problem with a lot of young athletes, musicians, or students is they lack one key character trait pertaining to greatness—patience. Too many of our children are getting discouraged and quitting what they initially loved to do at alarming rates because they are running toward a destination rather than realizing that performance is a journey, ever evolving and changing.

Imagine competing in a mile race and thinking to yourself, *This isn't so bad; I'm going to give it everything I have,* and you finish the race and are proud of yourself. But one tiny problem: it's not really a mile you were asked to run as you had thought—it's really 26.2 miles! You would most likely be discouraged, disappointed, and unmo–tivated to even try to run just over twenty–five more miles. Many people struggle to finish what they start because they think *success* is just around the corner, when in reality it's years down the road.

In this chapter I'm going to help you teach your child to enjoy the journey, keep her feet moving, and redefine success.

FOCUS ON THE PROCESS AND LET
THE RESULTS TAKE CARE OF THEMSELVES

Have you ever been in a store and seen a little kid screaming at the top of his lungs because he doesn't get what he wants? Sometimes we fall into the trap of doing the same thing when we don't immediately get what we want. Help your children understand that the road to excellence isn't for the faint of heart or for the impatient; performance excellence is going to take time. If they can develop the ability to focus on the process by focusing on the things they can control and let the results take care of themselves, their capacity to manage obstacles will be enhanced.

I'm not saying that results don't matter—because they do! There's nothing wrong if your children thrive to be victorious, but try to avoid making them feel bad if all they want to do is be in first place—legendary performers love to win. However, when your child becomes consumed with results, this inhibits her enjoyment of the journey. I've seen too many young athletes press the panic button because they are going through a little slump. If you see your child give less effort when she is losing or doubts her ability because she's not achieving "success" in the moment, it's most likely time for a mind–set check to help him be more process oriented as opposed to being fixated on the results.

MELISSA'S MIND-SET TRANSFORMATION

As you can probably tell from the introduction of this chapter, my wife, Melissa, is an athletic woman. Before we had children, our spare time together consisted of playing volleyball, tennis, and other sports. Little did we know that when Melissa got pregnant, it would trigger a slew of medical complications leaving her bedridden and emotionally downtrodden. After Melissa gave birth to our youngest daughter, she was left with fifty extra pounds. A few weeks passed, and that extra baby weight wasn't going to be temporary unless she did something about it, so she got to work.

For three years, Melissa tried diet after diet, put hours in at the gym, and did everything possible to shed the weight, but to no avail. It's frustrating when your best efforts yield no fruits, and this was the case for Melissa. One day she decided to stop focusing on a destination and start focusing on the journey. To do this, she did something that changed everything—she threw away the scale.

Refusing to allow a number to define success was the best decision she made when it comes to her health. Melissa hasn't stepped on a scale for years, and since deciding to stop keeping tabs of how much she weighs, she's completed a marathon, run a 5K, conquered a sprint triathlon (she had to learn how to swim to compete in it), did a thirty-five-mile bike race, volunteers to help women get in shape, and maxed the US Army Physical Fitness Test by doing eighty-five push-ups (in two minutes), doing ninety-three sit-ups (in two minutes), and running two miles in less than fifteen minutes. If you ask her why she does all this, her answer is simple: she loves it—the purest most effective form of motivation.

Melissa doesn't consider herself to be a fitness expert, nor does she go around advising people to do what she does. She acknowledges that everyone is different, and measuring weight might be helpful for other people, but it is just not for her. Her recipe for personal success when it comes to fitness is simple: *Focus on the process and let the results take care of themselves.*

IF THEY'RE PLAYING FOR FUN, LET THEM PLAY FOR FUN

If you're a parent or a coach (chances are you are if you're reading this book), brace yourself for what I'm about to write. Parents and coaches are the ones who get in the way of the kids' enjoyment of the journey. It's a shame to see adults fighting in the stands, coaches yelling at their players, and game officials getting an earful for blowing a call. All this happens at your local youth leagues. Sometimes parents will treat their children like they are professionals at what they do and take the fun out of their performance.

I saw a dad ruin the enjoyment his three-year-old was having while playing baseball in the living room by getting too technical with his swing. "Put your hands back," "Take your hands to the ball," and "Spread your legs" were all phrases this father was barking out while he was trying to coach his little boy to the ideal swing. The more he tried to tell his son what to do, the worse his son got, and the worse his son got, the more frustrated the dad became. The kid was just minding his own business swinging the bat for one purpose: to have fun (not to have the perfect swing). This dad I'm talking about is yours truly. It didn't take long before I realized what I was doing, so I decided to care less about what my son's swing looked like and more about putting a smile on his face.

The ironic thing is that one day I was watching ESPN experts breaking down the swing of Anaheim's Albert Pujols. They were showing his swing from many different angles and repeating it over and over again. My son, who enjoys impersonating people he sees, grabbed his bat, stood in front of the television screen, and said, "Like this, Daddy?" and then took a beautiful swing. I was so impressed that I made him do it again and again, and with every swing I got more excited. Like any proud father, I needed validation. "Son?" I asked. "Who taught you how to swing like that?" To my surprise, he turned around and pointed at Albert Pujols on the screen. "He did!"

If it's results you're after, help your children focus on having fun, and keep in mind that it's not fun to be corrected on every little thing they do wrong. As you let your children enjoy what they do, they'll be more relaxed, and when they're relaxed, they're in the best position to perform at a higher level.

THE LITTLE TEAM THAT COULD

After finishing my college baseball career, I went into coaching young baseball players. Although I worked with baseball players at all levels, I particularly enjoyed training young players learning how to play the game. When the time was right, I agreed to take the role as head coach for a select 10U baseball team called Ultimate Sports. My little team lacked pitching, defense, offense, and base-running skills, but they had great attitudes, and that's what made us dangerous.

Our first three months of playing as a team were difficult because we were losing by football scores—21–3, 17–0, and 24–5, just to list a few final scores off the top of my head. After every game during our team huddle, I would open the huddle with the same question:

"What did you learn in today's game?" Getting our shorts handed to us game after game wasn't fun, but if we were going to take a beating like that, we'd better be learning something that would make us better the next time. As a player and a parent, it's easy to let the score depict the level of fun the game is. Don't get me wrong. It's more fun to win, but when you're not winning, it's the coach's and parents' responsibility to teach the kids that there are other ways to measure success. No matter how much we lost by, I kept telling the boys (and the parents) that we weren't going to let the score dictate our effort level; we were going to continue to work hard at practice, have fun, and master the fundamentals.

By the time our first year ended, not only were we winning games, but we were also returning the favor to those teams who dominated us earlier in the season. It was special to have parents and coaches from the opposing team coming up to me after games, congratulating me for creating such an amazing turnaround. My response was always the same: "It's the parents."

It didn't matter if we were winning by ten or losing by ten; our mind–set was to play hard and always hustle, and the team had a blast doing so. As the coach of fourth– and fifth–graders, I found it easy to mold their minds and help them remain motivated. Making sure that the parents understand that it's not about winning and losing is another story. For parents to invest so much money for equipment, gas, hotels, and time for practice and tournaments, it makes sense that they would like to see their kids winning. The par–ents of the boys on my team were incredible. They supported each other's children, they supported their own children, and they let me do the coaching. As a parent, help your child enjoy the journey by keeping it fun, especially in the early stages of development.

Activity: Before every practice or performance, remind your child to have fun. The more fun she has, the more relaxed she is, which can enhance performance. Reminding your child to "have fun" might be a good reminder for yourself to do the same.

DON'T FORCE YOUR MIND-SET ON THEM

One day I grabbed a cup of hot chocolate with a man who wanted to know if it was possible to instill a killer instinct in his ten–year–old daughter. She was already a talented and competitive gymnast, but this loving father wondered if replacing her "this is fun" mentality with the "let's win this thing" mentality would help her succeed even more.

The answer: *Everyone is different. The key is to find the* right *mentality for your child.*

Some athletes like to joke around before a game, and some don't even like to smile; some get pumped up listening to rap, and some by listening to Justin Bieber. Some people need to get hyped before a performance, and others are doing their best to stay as calm as possible. Everyone is different, so you need to help your child figure out what works best for them and how to have the right mind–set at the right time.

TWO MIND-SETS

In the last chapter, I wrote about the difference between the *fixed* and *growth* mind–sets, but in this section I'm going to talk about the *results* versus *task* mind–sets. Kids that are more results oriented are very competitive. You're going to see that they love to win and get mad (sometimes a little too much) when things don't go their way during a performance, and a lot of their success is tied to how their performance compares to their peers. Having a results–oriented mind–set isn't inherently a bad thing. We live in a society where one's *healthy* drive to win can enhance effort, increase focus, and strengthen resilience. However, as I've explained, those who are too focused on results are more susceptible to frustration, anxiety, and a lack of intrinsic motivation.

The task mind–set, on the other hand, is focused on mastery. Your child with the task mind–set usually doesn't care about the score or if she is doing better than anyone else. She enjoys what she is doing, and if you ask her why she participates in his sport, she'll probably say, "Because I love it" or "It's fun!" This is beneficial because she is less likely to get caught up in stats, bracket seedings, and how his opponents are doing. For people with the task mind—set, losing isn't that big of a deal because winning isn't that big of a deal either! The downside is that you're not going to see a sense of urgency from these folks, nor are you going to see a die—hard attitude to come back from a big deficit. Can you see the conflict that can arise when you have a result mind—set parent with a task mind—set child?

So here's what you do . . .

The last thing you want to do is to impose your killer instinct mind—set on your task—oriented child; however, by knowing which mind—set is most beneficial for her, you're going to be in a better position to help her use what works. First, informally ask your child to share a time she had the *most fun* participating in his sport. Then, do something that might be hard: just listen. Pay close attention to what she is describing. Was it during practice? Was it with the game on the line? Was it when the team won? Did it happen in the backyard when no one was around? She will be giving you pieces of evidence to which mind—set she has.

Second, choose a time your child was successful during a per—formance—a time she was "in the zone." Ask her to describe what he was thinking, how he felt, what he did, and so on. Again, pay attention to statements that elude to the results or task mind—set.

Third, identify a time your child struggled or failed. Ask her what she was thinking, her feelings about the experience, and if feelings of failure and/or embarrassment were present. You're look—ing for details. By now, you should have some good evidence as to which mind—set your child leans toward (you most likely already knew before you even asked her these questions).

Finally, you want to use your child's answers to develop a plan that helps her according to her mind—set. For example, if you have a results—oriented athlete, just know she is likely to put a lot of pres—sure on herself and may worry too much about her opponent. In this case, make sure the words you use don't add fuel to the fire by saying, "you *have* to win" or "so much is riding on this." Your child already knows that, so those words don't help her. Help her relax instead.

If your child is more task oriented, invite her to continue to have fun and that you enjoy watching her do what she loves. Be aware, results—oriented coaches can have a bad effect on task—oriented athletes. Your child is going to have to learn how to focus on why she loves her sport. It's going to be more difficult, but it's possible.

Parents, you are one of the most important (if not *the* most important) influences on the enjoyment and performance of your young child's athletic experience. Rather than change your child's mind—set, help her discover what works for her and how to use it to her benefit.

Activity: Help your child discover the ideal mind-set she needs to enjoy the journey by following this four-step process:

(1) Help her identify a time she had the most fun performing (not necessarily a time she performed successfully).

(2) Identify when she performed at her best.

(3) Identify a time she performed poorly.

(4) Use what she said in each step to purposely craft a mind-set that will help her enjoy what she does.

ESPECIALLY FOR COACHES

AT THE TIME OF WRITING THIS BOOK, ONE OF THE most talked–about videos in the media was that of the now former head coach of the Rutgers men's basketball team shov–ing his players, kicking them, calling them derogatory names, and even throwing balls at them. Ultimately he was fired, but that sparked a thought: how many high school coaches, youth coaches, and even parents are doing this without anyone knowing?

The target audience for this book is parents who are trying to help their children develop the mental aspect of their game. How–ever, I also understand that you parents are also often the coaches of your children's teams. To help you with that, I've dedicated this chapter to help you succeed in one of your most influential roles you'll have—that of a coach.

IT'S NOT EASY BEING A COACH

The moment you decide (or are strongly encouraged) to be a coach, you are deciding to shape the minds of those youngsters you lead. Some of you are knowledgeable in your sport and have the strategic prowess comparable to coaches at higher levels; and some of you have no idea what you're doing, have never played that sport, and you are a coach only because no one else would do it!

Either way, I want to thank you for choosing to be an influence on the lives of our children. As a coach, I know that you're not only concerned about wins and losses, but you're also dealing with scheduling, playing time for each kid, coming up with the ideal strategy, and, hardest of all, dealing with the parents. It's not an easy job! Here are some principles to remember that will help you make it a successful season, regardless of your record.

START WITH A PURPOSE

Set yourself up for success by having a great first parents meeting. Your players' parents should know your coaching philosophy and what your goals are for the season. They should know your team rules, your philosophy on playing time, your communication with them, punctuality, and anything else you want to establish early. Help them understand that parental support is going to be the backbone to the team's success. They should feel comfortable talking to you, and it would be helpful to establish immediately that you have their children's best interests in mind.

PRACTICE ON PURPOSE

Your team's confidence is built on the practice field. Make sure you have a practice plan and that your assistant coaches know what you're going to be doing as well. Keep in mind that longer practices don't equate to better practices necessarily. Keep them short, make sure they're high intensity, and encourage your team to hustle at all times.

MASTER THE AFTER-GAME SPEECH

Remembering that sports are one of the best vehicles to teach life lessons will help you make connections from what happened in the game to how your team can use that experience to make them better students, siblings, and children. Regardless of the outcome of the game, make sure you highlight what went well and what the team can do to improve. This is a good time to point out the small successes players had that nobody else saw.

COMMUNICATE WITH THE KIDS

The players on your team are also dealing with things at home, the rigors of school, drama with friends, or even bullies. Each of these factors play into their ability to focus, the effort level they give, or the attitude they have on any given day. Before practice, talk to them individually and find out what they love to do, what their favorite video game is, where they like to eat, and so on.

CONTROL YOUR EMOTIONS

As a coach, you set the tone. It's a shame to see coaches who have no control of their emotions when it comes to communicating with their players or the game officials. Don't get me wrong. I'm not opposed to questioning a call or letting your frustration be known; however, *how* you do it is important. I've seen some great coaches get their point across by showing obvious frustration but doing it in a way that isn't condescending.

A leader that cannot control his or her emotions is not going to have the capacity to make good decisions when the game is on the line. Keep a cool head under pressure, and you'll be teaching a great lesson to everyone watching.

COMMUNICATE WITH THE PARENTS

Parents are going to make or break your team, so get to know them. Invite them to help out at practice and teach them the fundamentals of your sport so they can coach their children when they're at home. If you're having problems getting to know one of your players, talk to his parents, and they'll help you out. It's all about the kids, and if coaches and parents are working together to make it a great experience for the players, they're going to be in a great position to succeed on and off the field.

PLAY TO WIN

I'm a firm believer that you should play to win. Let me explain what I mean. Sometimes coaches will have the "let's just play for fun" mentality and won't teach their players the proper fundamentals and essential strategies to be victorious. Playing to win causes your players to perform at a high level under pressure, and those who can do this have a tremendous advantage in all aspects of their lives. As you have read in this book, "playing to win" doesn't mean winning at any cost; it means giving your players high expectations and providing the training necessary for them to succeed.

BUILD THEM WITH YOUR WORDS

You've heard the phrase "Sticks and stones can break my bones, but words will never hurt me." Well, that's false! The words coaches use can uplift or destroy. Effective praise is crucial to helping your players develop confidence in the early stages of their athletic careers. The first seven years are known as the "romance" years. It's in these developmental seasons that the *love* your players acquire for their sport will play a tremendous role in their likelihood to stick with it into their high school years, and your role as a coach has a lot of influence on how much they enjoy that sport.

When you see your players do something special, make sure you verbalize it and be specific. The specificity of your praise does two things: first, it shows your authenticity—a flippant "good job" can only go so far—and second, it gives your players a repeatable behavior to use as a standard.

GIVE EFFECTIVE CRITICISM

Your players are going to mess up. They're going to miss easy shots, make mental errors, and forget about practice; but how you choose to respond as a coach will teach volumes. Just like giving effective praise, being specific is also a key characteristic to giving effective criticism. How you make corrections is also important. If your players fear you or have resentment toward you, your message is going to be forgotten. If your players messes up, refuse to hold it over their heads for a prolonged period. Give them a chance to learn their lesson and move on. Remain in control when a player does something to frustrate you.

PREPARE THEM

The more prepared your players feel, the more confident they will be. I'll never forget my dad teaching our team what to do if we are on defense and two base runners are standing on the same base. He told us to tag the one who was originally occupying the bag and shout, "You're out!" (According to the rules, he's not really out.) Then tag the other runner and shout, "You're out!" (this runner is *really* out). Then when the first runner walks away because he thought he was out, tag him again and yell, "Now you're out!" We actually practiced this numerous times!

Months later, my team was playing at AAU Nationals against one of the best teams in the country in Sarasota, Florida. Wouldn't you know it that the other team had two base runners on the same base! My teammate ran over to them, tagged the first one—"You're out!"—then the second—"You're out!"—and like clockwork, the first one started walking toward the dugout, and my teammate tagged him again. "Now you're out!" It was a double play! All of us players laughed because it happened exactly like Coach said it would.

If your players are prepared for the playing conditions—the weather, how early or late the competition will be, and so on—they will be more likely to rise to the occasion. Before you do conditioning with them, tell them how difficult it will be and how they will have the inclination to want to give up but that they shouldn't give in. The best coaches prepare their players for worst-case scenarios and have a plan on how to make adjustments.

One of the best compliments I've received came from a teenager I was working with for years before he graduated high school. He walked up to me and, with a smile on his face, said, "I don't need you anymore." He was trying to communicate to me that he'd learned to identify his own routines, he knew what to do when adversity strikes, and he knew how to succeed when he wasn't at the top of his game. It was his way of telling me, "Thanks for everything, Coach."

ESPECIALLY FOR
PARENTS OF ATHLETES

THE DAY BEFORE MY SON'S FIRST T-BALL GAME, I decided to take him to the park for some quality father–son time to teach him the basics of baseball. (I probably shouldn't have waited until the day before his game to teach him how to play.) We started by playing catch, and then we moved to fielding ground balls, and then it came time to hit.

As we went from drill to drill, I noticed an interesting phenomenon: the more instruction I gave, the worse he got! It falls precisely in line with Tim Gallwey's book *The Inner Game of Tennis,* in which he claims that those just learning a sport do better by seeing the behavior rather than being told how to do it. It got to the point where I would do something, and then I would invite him to "do what Daddy did." It should have come as no surprise to see how quickly he picked it up.

Another valuable lesson I pulled from training with my five–year–old son is the effect enjoying the experience has on perfor–mance. I was testing out all of my verbal cues with him during our little batting practice: "keep the bat up," "swing quick," "be strong," and so on. I tried to keep these phrases short, instructional, and productive. While none of these statements produced tremendous results, one statement seemed to elicit a significantly different effect: "This is fun." The more I reminded him of how much fun he was having, the more relaxed he got. I taught him that he didn't *have to* hit the ball. He didn't *have to* have the perfect swing. He didn't even *have to* play baseball at all. My only invitation to him was to have fun and enjoy the experience of playing the game.

Parents make or break the success of a youth team. As a parent, no one wants your child to succeed more than you do, and, on some occasions, you may want your child to succeed more than she actually does. Sometimes your desire to see her live up to her potential can get in the way, and your overzealous actions actually drive your child away from wanting to play. I've seen many youth who only play their sport because it's what Mom and Dad want them to do, and not necessarily because they enjoy it. Here are some principles to remember that will help you help them.

ACTIONS SPEAK LOUDER THAN WORDS

If you want to help your child be at the top of her game, you must walk the talk. I once heard a quote that said, "Your actions are so loud that I cannot hear what you're saying."

DON'T USE FEAR OR EXTERNAL REWARDS AS MOTIVATORS

Giving your child an ultimatum or the rewards for a job well done undermines her intrinsic motivation. As you learned in the chapter about motivation, those strategies may work, but are only temporary and will do more damage than good in the long run.

IF YOU HAVE SOMETHING BAD TO SAY ABOUT YOUR CHILD'S COACH, KEEP IT TO YOURSELF

I'm not saying not to share it with *anyone*; you should be able to let out your frustration and even anger if you need to (at the right time and in the right place, of course). But a common trap many parents fall into is sharing their disdain for their child's coach or other parents with their child. This makes it difficult for the kid to respect the coach if he is receiving mixed messages from Mom and Dad. Again, we want the child to have fun and enjoy the game. It's hard to do if your child senses animosity between you and the coach; if it does happen, keep it civil.

HELP THEM LOVE THE GAME

As said previously, the first years of children's athletic development in any sport is what we in sport psychology call "the romance stage." It's called the romance stage because this is when they begin to develop a love for their sport. As children get older, training gets more rigorous, the stakes get higher, and the pressure to perform increases. The athletes who are going to stick around for their high school years (and even after) are the ones who developed a love for their sport at an early age. You can help young athletes develop this love by protecting them from getting too caught up in statistics, results, and the drama happening between the parents. Let them dream, and allow them to say, "I want to be a professional athlete when I grow up," or "I'm going to play [insert sport] in college." You might know that their genetics aren't in their favor or you might not want them to pursue that dream, but as your children, they want your support and not your doubts. For some youngsters it might just be a fleeting phase in their lives, while for others it is an actual pursuit. In either case, although the chances are slim that your child will ever become a professional athlete, she will be able to look back and see that a constant in their journey was the support from Mom and Dad.

TEACH THEM THAT FAILING IS SOMETHING THAT HAPPENS, NOT SOMETHING THEY ARE

The best coaches allow their players to fail without letting them feel like failures. We live in a time where everyone gets a trophy because we don't want to hurt anyone's feelings. These kids are going to experience failure in many aspects of their lives, and there's no better place than the athletic field to teach these children how to learn from their failures, control their emotions, and keep moving forward.

LESS INSTRUCTING

I saw a kid with a nice little swing completely struggle the moment he got to the plate. Everyone in the stands became his coach: "Keep your elbow up!" "Keep your eye on the ball!" "Don't hit it in the air!" "Don't do that with your foot!" Poor kid. He looked paralyzed up there swinging the bat. Barking out instructional commands to children who don't fully understand the game, aren't very athletic, and can't control their bodies well might not be the best way to help them in their moment of performance. Now, I'm not saying to *never* instruct your child during a game. Practice is the best time to do the instructing, and doing it during a game isn't necessarily a bad time to teach skills. But keep it to a minimum so your child doesn't have to think so much. Yogi Berra once said, "It's impossible to hit and think at the same time." I agree.

MORE PRAISING

While we want to decrease our dosage of instructions, the thing parents and coaches should do more of is give effective praise. Tell the youngsters what they're doing well, and rather than just say, "good job," tell them why. Saying that extra sentence shows your authenticity and makes the behavior more replicable—especially if you focus on the things they can control.

MASTER THE CAR-RIDE-HOME TALK

Have you done this . . . after a bad game your child gets into the car and you express your frustration with him immediately? This isn't the best idea for two reasons: (1) you might not be as composed as you need to be to share constructive criticism, and (2) your child is still too emotional to think clearly. Give it some time before you share your thoughts. The best thing you can do is listen. On many occasions, your child will initiate the conversation and give you her opinion on how the performance went. As you know, the great majority of what's going to be coming out of your child's mouth will be negative. Let it be. Allow your child to vent without being quick to give your opinion or explain why his opinion is wrong. Just listen. What your child is saying will reveal how he is interpreting her situation, and this will serve her (and you) well to capture this information and use it to help her next time. Master your ability to ask effective questions to help her gain a better understanding of what just happened.

On those amazing performances, make sure you help her multiply the success! The car ride isn't the time to talk about improvements; just embrace everything your child did well. Ask questions like, "What where you thinking when . . ." or "How did you prepare for this performance?" Help her discover what she did so she can replicate it at the next performance. Make sure you praise the hard work, focus, and effort your child put forth to achieve those great results—*not* the result itself.

HELP YOUR CHILD DEVELOP ROUTINES

Help your child develop pregame, during the game, and a post-game routine to develop consistency in the way she thinks and performs.

SOMETIMES NO WORDS ARE THE BEST WORDS

If you're that parent who has to instruct every second, try to bite your tongue. Let the child make mistakes and correct them on her own. Sometime silence can be used as a great teacher, especially if the child is older.

GET TO KNOW THE OTHER PARENTS AND CHEER FOR THEIR KIDS

This is a simple gesture, but it has a powerful effect on the entire team. I love hearing all of the parents support not only their own children but also the other players as if they were their own.

DON'T TRY TO MIND READ BUT SEEK TO UNDERSTAND

One of the quickest ways to get your child to stop talking to you is to tell him what he is thinking. I heard an exchange between a father and a son after a game once. The father was adamant that the reason the son had a bad game was because his mind was on what he was going to do after the game. The young man kept telling his father to stop acting like he knew what he was thinking, and the conversation continued to escalate. Not once did I hear the father ask his son anything; all he did was tell him what he *knew* his son was thinking.

DON'T MAKE IT BIGGER THAN IT REALLY IS

This is a common pitfall for parents. A child will be ready for the big tournament or competition, and just before he goes out to play, the parent says, "I'm so nervous for you!"; "The other team is amazing!"; "If you mess up, you're not going to be able to win"; and other pressure–intensifying statements. Help your child keep her sport in perspective.

YOUR GO-TO GUIDE
FOR GAME DAY

T HE DAY OF YOUR CHILD'S COMPETITION HAS ARRIVED, and chances are you're probably just as nervous as he is (some of you may even be more nervous). What can you do as a parent to help him perform at his best when it matters most? Here are nine principles to remember:

1. Help your child remember his purpose

When the pressure is on, it's easy to get lost in the hype of the moment. Your child will perform at his best when he remembers what defines success for him. Help him remember why he plays that sport; remembering this will help him stay locked—in to what mat—ters most.

2. See it before it happens

Before the game, tell your child to visualize two things: (1) what he wants to happen, and (2) what he's going to do about it. Tell him to see the performance happen before he even shows up to the venue. Mental rehearsal is one of the most important mental skills to practice before a competition.

3. Learn how to take a hit

Remind your child that adversity is going to happen. He might make an error, he could fall, an official might make a bad call, or he might even sit the bench. Set your child up for success by having a game plan for what he's going to do when those things happen. Arm your child with a bounce–back plan to performance setbacks. The better his plan is, the quicker he can get his head back into the game. The truth about the zone is that it's overrated! It's not over–rated because it doesn't exist; it's overrated because the majority of your child's performances will not be in the zone! The best com–petitors aren't the one's who always have their "A game"; they're the ones who find a way to be successful when they have their B, C, or D games.

4. Make sure your child knows what he wants

Have your child come up with a mission for the moment. This can be something simple and process oriented. I had a cheerleader tell me that her mission was to "have fun"; a golfer I told me he was going to "focus on breathing"; and an ice skater was going to "smile" throughout the competition. Each of these athletes knew that by focusing on these things, it was symbolic to them that they were in control.

5. Make sure your child focuses on the controllable

Your child gives power to what you focus on, so make sure his focus is centered on the controllable. He has no power over the other competitors, what people think about him, his equipment, the weather, and so on. If he's not careful, he can get lost giving attention to the ineffective "what ifs"—"What if I don't do well? What if I get injured? What if I don't finish?" If he's going to play the "what–if" game with himself, make sure they don't forget the positive what–ifs: "What if I have the best performance ever? What if I finish way faster than I imagined?"

6. Help your child master his self-talk

Thoughts affect our emotions, which affect our body (heart rate, muscle tension, breathing, and so on), which affects our performance. Studies show that we say anywhere from three hundred to one thousand words to ourselves per minute, and these words have a tremendous influence on how we perform. Help your child develop an arsenal of words, phrases, people, or images he can think of that will help him stay strong throughout the competition.

7. Focus on the process

The most important moment of each competition is the present. Remind your child to lose himself in the "here and now." As he focuses on *one* pitch at a time, *one* possession at a time, *one* serve at a time, or *one* shot at a time, he becomes more likely to shut off the mental chatter and be fully absorbed in his performance.

8. Be greedy with your child's energy

Hopefully your child knows what his energy-level needs to be at to perform at an optimal level. I always ask my students, "On a relaxation scale between one and ten, what number are you when you are performing at your best (ten being extremely pumped and one being extremely relaxed)?" It's important your child knows his number because it's *his* job to not only be aware of his energy level but also, more important, to regulate it by eating the right things, breathing correctly, listening to the right music, and even thinking effectively.

9. Let the nerves happen

Your child is going to be nervous, experience butterflies, and have a racing heart before he even gets started—and that's okay! It's his body telling him that he's ready to perform and it's showtime. Too many people get nervous because they're nervous—go figure! Tell your child to embrace the nerves, slow his breathing, and smile because he's ready for this moment.

When your child is performing at his best, he is doing certain things and not doing certain things. Pay close attention to the little things he might do unknowingly that might hinder or help his performance. Sports are humbling, but consistent performance is preceded by consistent preparation and thinking.

[CONCLUSION]

POSTGAME MEETING

EVERY NIGHT WE HAVE A ROUTINE IN THE SU'A household. Before the kids go to sleep, I go to each of their beds to tuck them in. The routine is exactly the same: I ask them three questions, I tell them how special they are to us, we pray together, and then I tickle them for a few seconds—in that exact order, every night.

You've been given a lot of information within the pages of this book. And to reiterate what I mentioned in the introduction, I don't expect you to use all of it. The key is to keep it simple. As I close, I wish to leave you with the same three questions I ask my children every night before the close of each day.

QUESTION #1: WHAT WAS SOMETHING GOOD THAT HAPPENED TODAY?

One night when I asked my son this question, he said, "I accidentally kissed a girl at school." The kid is six years old, and he's talking about "accidentally" kissing girls at school? I wasn't buying it. His story was that he was spinning in circles and was so dizzy that he ran into a girl, apparently lips first—yeah right. After showing interest in his unofficial first-kiss story, I told him no more accidental kissing, to which he agreed, and then we moved on to the next question.

Help your child flex her optimistic muscles often. It's easy to be negative, and the better she gets at identifying what is going well, the more resilience she will have. The more she is asked to share the bright spots he experiences every day, the more aware she will become.

QUESTION #2: WHAT DID YOU LEARN TODAY?

One night Mya told me that she learned that it was important to be honest. I was pleasantly surprised by her response and asked her how she learned that. She told me that she was listening to me reprimand Jarom (her big brother) earlier that day when he failed to tell the truth. She wasn't even in the room, but she was listening, and, more important, she was learning.

Help your child develop a desire to continue to learn about her-self. He should always be learning. After each practice, each game, each day at school, a good question to ask is, "What did you learn today?" As your children train themselves to learn, they will go into each day with the attitude to improve.

QUESTION #3: WHAT'S ONE THING YOU ARE GOING TO DO BETTER TOMORROW?

I was out of town on business one night, so Melissa tucked the kids in. While talking to our youngest daughter, Eliana, Melissa asked, "What are you going to do better tomorrow, sweetheart?" "I don't know," little Eli answered. Melissa made a suggestion. "How about be really kind and loving to your brother and sister tomorrow by sharing and being nice to them?" Eliana thought about Melissa's proposition and replied, "No, I think I want to take a break from all of that for a while."

No matter how bad we want our children to do something, in the long run, it has to be their choice. However, helping your son or daughter choose to improve *one* thing every day is manageable and doable. Before each day, having your children ask themselves, "What's one thing I'm going to do better today?" can have tremen-dous benefits if they run with it.

A LESSON ABOUT PARENTING TAUGHT TO ME BY MY SON

One day Melissa and I were in the kitchen talking when Jarom, out of nowhere, came into the kitchen, walked up to Melissa, gave her a big hug and a gentle kiss on the cheek, and expressed a sincere "I love you, Mommy." Melissa was both touched and surprised by this kind unexpected gesture from our little guy. As he was walk-ing away, he stared at me with a little smirk on his face, as if to say, "That's *my* mommy." I stopped him before he left and asked, "What was that all about, son? Why did you do that?" Then he said the words I'll never forget: "I do what I see you do, Daddy."

My concluding message is simple. When it comes to teaching mental skills to your children, the power to teach is founded by your example of using them yourself. In order to teach your children to be more optimistic, I invite you to practice seeing the good side of things as well. To help your children overcome thoughts of inad-equacy, I invite you to help them not only see who they are today, but who they can become.

I hope you can use the skills and strategies taught in this book to help your children own their thoughts so they can own their emotions, behaviors, and ultimately their performance. High per-formers have great habits. Identify which habits are getting in your child's way, and remind her to be patient as she continues to evolve into the athlete, student, musician, dancer, or leader she is striving to be.

I've been a part of many championship teams and have worked with world-class organizations, but regardless of how great each of these teams were or how successful they may have been, one thing will always remain true: the most important team you and I will ever be a part of is our family.

ABOUT
THE AUTHOR

J USTIN SU'A IS A SPORT AND PERFORMANCE PSYCHOL-
ogy consultant and Head of Mental Conditioning at the IMG
Academy, the world–leading provider of athletic and personal
development training programs for youth, adult, collegiate, and pro–
fessional athletes, located in Bradenton, Florida. He's a member of
the Association for Applied Sport Psychology (AASP) and completed
his master's degree in exercise science with an interest in the nature
of peak performance from the University of Utah. Justin's students
perform in the NFL, in the Olympics, on *Dancing with the Stars*, at
Division I universities, and in numerous business corporations. He's
also worked with the American Samoa National Olympic Com–
mittee and the United States military. Justin was a Freshman All–
American pitcher at Brigham Young University. Most importantly,
he is a husband and a father of three wonderful children.

0 26575 12845 1